SSENTIAL LEGAL SKILLS

Advocacy

Andy Boon

Series Editor
JULIE MACFARLANE

Cavendish
Publishing
Limited

First published in Great Britain 1993 by Cavendish Publishing Limited, 23A Countess Road, London NW5 2XH.

Telephone: 071-485 0303 Facsimile: 071-485 0304

British Library Cataloguing in Publication Data

Boon, A
Advocacy - (Essential Legal Skills Series)
I Title II Series
340.023

ISBN 1-874241-42-2

Cover photograph by Jerome Yeats
Printed and bound in Great Britain

Contents

9   Advocacy in practice 2   **175**

10   Evaluation and reflection   **189**

Editor's Introduction

'The essence of our lawyer's craft lies in skills ...; in practical, effective, persuasive, inventive skills for getting things done ...'

Karl Llewellyn

The appearance of this new series of texts on legal skills reflects the recent shift in emphasis in legal education away from a focus on teaching legal information and towards the teaching and learning of task-related and problem-solving skills.

Legal education in the United Kingdom has undergone significant changes over the past ten years as a result of growing concern, expressed for the most part by the profession, over its adequacy to prepare students for the practice of law. At the same time, many legal educators have voiced fears that concentrating on drilling students in substantive law promotes neither the agility of mind nor the development of judgment skills which provide the basis for continued learning.

Today courses providing clinical experience and instruction in legal skills are increasingly a part of undergraduate law programmes. Both branches of the profession in England and Wales have fundamentally revised the content and format of their qualifying courses to include direct instruction in practical skills. In Scotland, the Diploma in Legal Practice, which emphasises the learning of practical skills, has been in place since 1980/81.

Nonetheless, legal skills education in the United Kingdom is still in its infancy. Much is to be learned from other jurisdictions which have a longer history of the use of practical and experience-based teaching methods, lessons invaluable to UK law teachers many of whom now face the challenge of developing new courses on legal skills. The ready exchange of ideas between skills teachers in the United Kingdom and abroad is an important part of the development process. So too is the generation of 'home-grown' texts and materials designed specifically for legal skills education in undergraduate and professional schools in the United Kingdom.

The introduction of skills teaching into the legal education curriculum has implications not only for what students learn in law school but also for how they learn. Similarly it has implications for the kind of textbooks which will be genuinely useful to students who wish to succeed in these programmes.

This new series of texts seeks to meet this need. Each text leads the reader through a stage-by-stage model of the development of a particular legal skill; from planning, through implementation in a variety of guises, to evaluation of performance. Each contains numerous practical exercises and guides to improve practice. Each draws on a network of theories about effective legal practice and relates theory to practice where that is useful and relevant.

The authors are all skills teachers with many years of practical experience at all levels of legal education. They draw on relevant literature and practice from all over the common law world. However each book is written specifically for students of law and legal practice in the United Kingdom and sets learning in the context of English law and against the backdrop of the Law Society's standards for the new Legal Practice Courses, due to commence in 1993/4.

Each of these texts is designed for use either as a supplement to a legal skills course taught at an undergraduate or professional level, or as a model for the structure and content of the course itself. We recommend the use of these books, therefore, to students and skills teachers alike, and hope that you enjoy them.

Julie Macfarlane
London, Ontario
February 1993

Acknowledgements

I would like to thank friends and colleagues who have helped in the preparation; Susan Nash, Derek O'Brien from the University of Westminster, Tim Maloney of Simmonds Church Smiles and fellow author Jenny Chapman were particularly helpful in relation to aspects of procedure. My partner, Helen, put in many hours as a 'lay reader' and the series editor, Julie MacFarlane, made many constructive, sensible and essential suggestions. Finally, I would like to acknowledge Cavendish Publishing for their support, patience and encouragement. Needless to say, any errors of omission or commission are my own.

Andy Boon
March 1993

Introduction

'The only thing to do with good advice is to pass it on; it is never any use to oneself.'

Oscar Wilde

There are many reasons why advocacy is a skill worth mastering. Understanding the task of the advocate in presenting a case for trial is central to understanding the litigation process. Understanding advocacy helps a lawyer to prepare cases for others to present. It enables her to give realistic, cogent and confident advice to her clients. Aspiring solicitors may not want to practise as an advocate, assuming this to be the job of the barrister. You will lead a very sheltered life as a solicitor if you are never required to make any kind of court appearance. If this day comes you will want to do a good job.

Even if you never appear as an advocate you may want to instruct one; understanding advocacy, you will be better able to evaluate the advocates you see and recommend one who is best suited to speak on behalf of your client. Advocacy is about persuading people; you cannot go through life without, on occasions, needing to persuade. Advocacy is often useful, and sometimes vital, in client interviewing, in negotiation and in meetings, client seminars and public lectures. If you do not practice law at all, principles of advocacy will be useful in whatever you do; advocacy is a valuable skill, a transferable skill, a lifelong skill.

For over 2000 years people have analysed, theorised and written about the subject. Contexts change but many of the basic principles, espoused by Aristotle, Cicero, and Quintillian seem to endure. Only recently have research findings begun to influence the way we think about advocacy. Often this research is conducted in the United States and it usually considers the psychological impact of particular techniques on juries. The jury is, of course, a feature of civil as well as criminal cases in the United States. In researching material for this book I have drawn on North American materials because this research often confirms our feelings about what is, or is not, effective. Nevertheless, there are many books on advocacy by contemporary advocates. These are often in broad agreement about the role and impact of advocacy as practised in our domestic courts. Many draw on examples from the last 100 years. During that time the common law tradition has produced many outstanding advocates. The cases in which they appear repay study by the intending practitioner. Indeed, extracts from a trial of Alfred Arthur Rouse, prosecuted by Sir Norman Birkett in 1931, will feature in this book. In 1948 Sir Norman said:

> *'I have been at the Bar and upon the bench for thirty four years and I have seen almost every kind of advocate in almost every type of court. And I know at once there are no standards that you can lay down and say, there is the pattern. It can't be done. There are diversities of gifts but there is the same spirit; and I have known in my time, men who could scarcely string a sentence together, who lacked all graces, and yet impressed the court so that the court strained to listen and to catch every word that was said'.*

'The Art of Advocacy:
Character and Skills for the Trial of Cases'
The Right Hon Sir Norman Birkett PC
American Bar Association Journal (1948) Vol 34

Nowadays, we are more confident that it is possible to train people to be competent advocates even if this does not lead to 'greatness'. In fact, most of the advocates who have been accorded that recognition have had particular strengths. It may be that to move into the realm of excellence the advocate requires some rare, indefinable talent, some strength of personality which cannot be taught. Identifying that quality of excellence, let alone teaching it, is not the purpose of this book.

Today, our mental picture of advocates is conditioned by images of the big and small screen, from films such as 'The Verdict' to television series like 'LA Law' or 'Rumpole of the Bailey'. The collage of impressions which drama produces is rooted in reality. Nevertheless, the picture is too glamorous and dramatic. In real life the vital witness seldom agrees to testify at the last minute, nor does he break down under cross examination and admit to lying.

The danger in dramatic role models is that they lead us to believe that advocacy is all to do with personality, flashy tricks and inspiration and little to do with careful thought and hard work. While 'great' advocates may be gifted in particular respects, most people can learn to do a competent job. If some of the great speakers of the past visited our courts today their oratory would seem out of place; they were great because they captured the mood and style of their time. Likewise, the style of speeches supporting acquittal on a murder charge may be inappropriate where the charge is drunken driving. While we can still learn from advocates of the past and present it is importance to recognise that effectiveness requires the ability to adapt to novel situations as much as it requires natural gifts. For this reason I am more concerned that this book encourages you to think about advocacy rather than tells you how to do it.

For most advocates starting out in the courts there will be very little drama, at least not of the kind which we see on the screen. While there may be times when an advocate needs to 'ham it up' she will always need to be a good technician; to understand the client's objectives, to analyse the extent to which the law can help to achieve these, to prepare the case and to present it in the most favourable way. The principles of good advocacy are not difficult to state and may even seem to be common sense. Like most good ideas they seem obvious with hindsight. The use of most techniques or devices depend on the demands of a situation; what may be the right thing to do in one situation may prove disastrous in another. Effective advocacy is not just about knowing the techniques but selecting from them as the situation demands. One writer suggests that an advocate needs 25 jury trials before he begins to become an effective advocate. Less complex hearings may demand fewer 'tries' but each performance must be subjected to thorough analysis if progress is to be made.

Personality may predispose advocates to a particular style. It may even produce advocacy suitable to a certain kind of case; those best suited to act for prosecutor or plaintiff, accused or defendant. An effective advocate needs to know the range of strategic choices which can be made in the pursuit of the client's goals. Many trainee solicitors' experience of advocacy in traineeship and after is of the 'in at the deep ending' training method. This often means being given a file at short notice and asked to 'do this summons'. In my own experience, nothing in my previous education had prepared me for the task. Nobody seemed willing or able to say how it should be done. 'It will all be clear from the summons' was the best I could expect. Preparation was inadequate because it was not clear what was being prepared for. While I sat in the Master's room in the High Court waiting for my case to be called I observed my contemporaries being grilled, humiliated and sent packing. Experience was hard won and, with no framework for evaluation, it was difficult to know how to improve. People who have gained their experience 'the hard way' can very quickly forget the pain they suffered in the process or the simple questions which concern the novice.

The aims of this book are to encourage you to:

- feel confident that you have planned your advocacy well

- have clear sight of your objectives and how to achieve them

- do a competent job of advocacy when required and that you can

- learn from your experiences of advocacy and do an even better job the next time and

- be conscious of your strengths and able to gain confidence from them

- be aware of your own limitations but not to be intimidated by them and
- analyse and, where possible, eliminate weaknesses

This book will be of practical assistance to undergraduate law students taking part in advocacy training exercises and moots. Students studying advocacy for the Legal Practice Course will study a course which differs according to the institution which offers it. The broad framework set out by the Law Society provides 'standards' for the competent performance of advocacy. These standards assume:

'... that the student should already have developed oral and written communication skills, interpersonal skills, and the skills of legal analysis and research. It is assumed, in particular, that a student should be able to:

- listen effectively
- engage in oral discussion in a clear and concise fashion
- record or summarise a discussion in clear and concise notes
- write clearly and precisely with attention to grammar, style organisation, bibliographies and citations
- work co-operatively in small groups
- extract, analyse and apply up to date law from primary sources, including case reports, primary and delegated legislation.'

In writing this book I have assumed that students will possess these basic competences. I have assumed, in particular, that you will be able to organise the activities suggested in the text.

As regards advocacy the Legal Practice Course requires that:

'The student should be able to formulate and present a coherent submission based upon facts, general principles and legal authority in a structured, concise and persuasive manner. The student should understand the crucial importance of preparation and the best way to undertake it. The student should be able to demonstrate an understanding of the basic skills in the presentation of cases before various courts and tribunals and should be able to:

1   identify the client's goals

2   identify and analyse factual material

3   identify the legal context in which the factual issue arises

4   relate the central legal and factual issues to each other

5   state in summary form the strengths and weaknesses of the case from each party's perspective

6   develop a presentation strategy

7   outline the facts in simple narrative form

8   structure and present in simple form the legal framework of the case

9   structure the submission as a series of propositions based on the evidence

10 identify, analyse and assess the specific communication skills and techniques employed by the presenting advocate

11 demonstrate an understanding of the purpose, techniques and tactics of examination, cross-examination and re-examination to adduce, rebut and clarify evidence

12 demonstrate an understanding of the ethics, etiquette and conventions of advocacy.'

Criteria 1-9 inclusive could all form part of a transaction leading to a performance in the form of a simple submission, such as an application by summons. Performance criteria 10-12 inclusive relate to the 'identification and analysis' of specific skills and the demonstration of understanding of their significance. Satisfying these criteria need not depend on an advocacy performance but on a paper exercise. 'Professional Conduct', one of the pervasive areas in the Legal Practice Course, may also appear in connection with advocacy. Professional conduct in relation to advocacy is dealt with in Chapter 3 of this book.

Competent performance will always depend on both legal knowledge and the skills which allow it to be applied. This is not a book on either law or legal procedure. It is a book which would be helpful in achieving entry level standards for the Legal Practice Course and a competent standard of advocacy in practice. However, elements of procedure are necessary to place practical advocacy in a meaningful context. Where I have found it necessary to mention procedure for this reason I have tried to keep this material to a minimum. Similar procedures constrain advocates in various courts. References to illustrative procedural or evidential rules are limited so as to maintain the focus on the essential skills of presenting a persuasive case. However, before appearing in any court or tribunal you should be familiar with the procedural and evidential rules which will govern the proceedings.

At the end of each Chapter I have included 'further reading' which I hope you find useful sources of these materials.

Andy Boon
March 1993

CHAPTER

1

Presenting to Persuade

1.1 Elements of persuasion

The advocate's task is threefold:-

1) To be heard; to be interesting; to engage the audience in the presentation

2) To get the message across; to select the right content and to emphasise the key points

3) To persuade the audience to the view advocated

Presentation skills are the key to persuasion because presentation carries the message. Aristotle identified three major elements of persuasion; ethos, pathos and logos.

Ethos

The speaker must convince the audience that she is trustworthy, credible, authentic and, in short, believable.

We can do this by telling the audience how important we are, how many degrees we hold or that we have experience in the area we are talking about. It is preferable for this to be done with humility. However, the audience is more likely to be impressed, and to accept us if, rather than parading our credentials, we are at ease with them, if we show that we know what we are talking about and, importantly, that we respect them.

Pathos

The speaker appeals to the emotions of the audience so that they are psychologically inclined to accept his argument. The significance of this element of persuasion depends on the cause which the speaker supports. Its relevance will be seen as we progress.

Logos

The speaker must provide reasoned argument as a foundation for that decision. The advocate's reasoned argument relates to the rules of law which, she claims, support her client's right to the court's decision.

1.2   A sense of audience

A presentation must be appropriate for an audience. Where a jury decides issues of fact the issues must be clearly presented to them in a way which will hold the jury members' interest. Lay magistrates may have little or no legal background. They might also appreciate a presentation of the case which is accessible and not overburdened with legal jargon. Court officials with legal backgrounds will be familiar with the language of the law; this does not mean that they are immune to the persuasion of the effective presenter. Many judges writing on their experience of the bench have made the point, and it is worth remembering, that judges are human too

> 'What is frequently overlooked is that non-jury cases are tried to a one man jury, that the juror in robes, like the juror in the box, is made of human material, possessed of the common virtues and the common frailties. He, too has to be kept interested. If he is sleeping he has to be aroused. He has to be persuaded. Your knowledge must become his knowledge, your inferences must be made his inferences. If you fail in these primary objectives you might as well keep your client at home and save the subpoena fees of your witnesses'.

Rifkind (1984)

1.3   Planning and organisation

There are many different ways of planning a presentation. The worst thing to do is to write down, word for word, what you intend to say. A presenter who has his eyes glued to his notes frequently has a boring delivery and is not persuasive. Imagine a salesperson who reads a patter from a prepared script; would you be convinced? When you read a script your voice generally lacks interest and your body movement is limited; both voice and body movement are crucial to effective presentation. Even when presenters have managed to free themselves from the tyranny of a script the average presentation is easily forgotten. Why? Anxiety can cause us to suppress our natural personalities. Audiences usually cause speakers to feel anxious; the larger, the more unfamiliar the audience or setting, the more anxious is the speaker and the greater the temptation to seek refuge in mediocrity. We are often so concerned about ourselves that we don't think enough about the audience and their needs.

> A logical device for avoiding reading a script is to plan by making a list of things we want to say. Outlining in this way is an improvement on scripting but it also has limitations if it is used inflexibly and without imagination. Planning for presentation is a creative activity. Outlining is time consuming and does not always encourage maximum creativity. It follows from our educational conditioning that we tend to rely on the organisational, logical parts of our brain while we write an outline (see 'Legal Writing' by Margot Costanzo, in this series). We tend to think about the first point to make whereas the first point may suggest itself at the end rather than the beginning of our planning. Because planning a presentation is a creative process it benefits from a method which releases creative potential.

> Gelb (1988)

Outline for presentation: the disadvantages of outlines

1 ~~You sit and think 'where to start?"~~

2 You have an idea but, by writing it down, it may not appear in the most logical place.

3 Outlines are therefore inflexible.

~~3~~ 1 Not creative.

~~2~~ 4 Temptation to add detail and make outline too long. This means that it may go over the page and begin to suffer from some of the same defects as a written speech:- ~~it it is not just a number of ideas but the outline becomes the text.~~

~~6~~ 5 Need to organise while writing.

~~7~~ 6 When you get to the end you probably want to change the order, add and delete, re-organise and re-number; you are more likely to tear the whole thing up?

~~8~~ 7 Relevance to advocacy (should this be the first point?)   ?

~~9~~ 8 Difficult to remember.

Mind map for presentation: the advantages of mind maps

Mind mapping is an alternative to outlining which is quick, fun and creative. It is a diagram of doodles and words which spread out from a central concept, the topic for the presentation. It puts you in the right frame of mind for an audience and releases creative energy. Mind maps are more easily changed and adapted than outlines. They are quicker to make and contain all the key points on one page. Because of this they can be more easily learned and remembered. Once you have refined your map you can learn it simply by reproducing it from memory. After a few tries you should have perfect recall off the elements of your mind map. Once you have produced your mind map, go back and think about your objectives for a particular presentation. These should be written out in full. Having organised them you should go back and see whether your mind map needs changing to achieve your objectives. The advantages of mind mapping are that you should approach your presentation having utilised all your creative energy in the planning process. Your content should be more diverse and interesting. Your presentation should be more diverse and interesting.

Mind Map for presentation: Advantages of mind maps

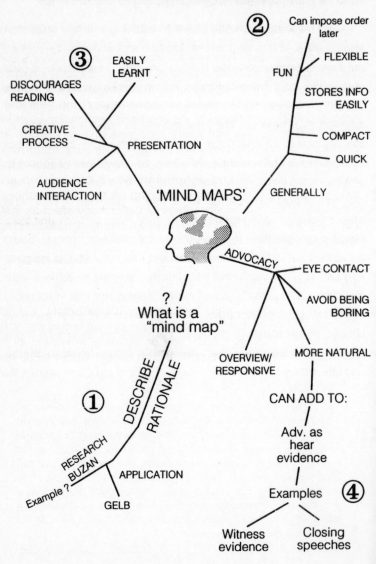

1.4   Structure and Organisation

There is a major principle of organisation which bears on every presentation; the clearest recollection is of those points which are made first and last. This is what North American lawyers call 'primacy' and 'recency'. The effect is illustrated by some research following a trial in Los Angeles which lasted six and a half months. At the beginning of the trial a representative of the defendant corporation was introduced to the court and remained in court for three days. After the trial every juror was able to provide an accurate description of that person. The jury members' recollection of later witnesses was poor; they even confused the experts for plaintiff and defendant. Why? Our senses are heightened by unfamiliarity. Depending on the circumstances, most speakers have the advantage of the primacy effect as they begin a presentation. To a lesser extent a clearly signalled ending will also stimulate an audience.

Vinson (1985)

1.5   Personal Style

Cultivating a personal style for advocacy is problematic. Do not assume that you must be a 'cardboard cut-out' advocate who must conform to some model. You do not need to know it all or pretend that you do. Be yourself and be honest. Above all do not feel as if you must always be 'right'. Richard Du Cann argues that an advocate

> '... must be convincing in his manner and with his material: yet concessions, hesitations and even self-corrections can lend an air of truth to his subsequent statements. There must be variety in his language and in the tone of his voice, he must avoid monotony like the plague: yet repetition of a word or phrase can be a valuable weapon. One part of the case may demand a rapid summary of fact, and another require him to dwell at length on a single point. His remarks might have relevance to the facts before the court; yet a healthy digression may enable him to return to the issues with a renewed force ...'

Du Cann (1980)

1.6   Voice

It is instinctive to respond to authoritativeness; we tend to associate this with a well modulated voice and calm but confident body movement. The ambition of the advocate in her presentation should be to sound sincere and authoritative without being pompous or arrogant. One of the problems of being anxious is that the quality of the voice is affected. Tension in the neck and diaphragm makes the voice higher than normal. Taking a sharp breath, a normal reaction to a threatening situation, can make you breathy and squeaky. All of these symptoms, which flatten out our voice so that it loses it natural highs and lows, can lead you to speak in a monotone. Be calm, measured and project your voice. Even if this is not how you feel, fake it until you have gained confidence.

Remember that if you look down you will lose projection; so either don't look down or don't speak while you do! The best advice is not to worry too much about your natural voice; if you try and change the way you speak or your pitch you will feel uncomfortable. If you feel confident in what you are doing your natural voice will be fine to start with and your delivery will improve with experience. If however you continue to experience problems many people have benefited by the Alexander technique for which you would need to join a class to get full benefit.

1.7   Words

The words we use are a powerful element in persuasion and yet words must be used with care. One person's orator is another's windbag. It is often said that an advocate should be eloquent. In abstract, eloquence is 'the art of fine speaking'. This begs the question 'what is fine speaking?' Eloquence is no more than the power of uttering strong emotion in appropriate, expressive and fluent language; in essence eloquence is using the power of persuasion. Eloquence must fit the occasion. Language which is inappropriate in a particular setting is embarrassing to the audience and is therefore likely to be ineffective.

One of the finest speeches ever made, 'The Gettysburg Address', is expressed in simple, powerful language.

> *'four score and seven years ago our fathers brought forth upon this continent a new nation, conceived in liberty, and dedicated to the proposition that all men are created equal ...'*

Complex language can obscure the message; direct language is often more effective because it is assertive. Speech behaviour analysis of successful prosecutors in the US found that the key characteristic was 'verbal assertiveness'. They tended to ask the witness more direct questions and made firm statements about the evidence in their speeches. Prosecutors securing fewer convictions were more polite, used careful grammar and made qualified statements in their speeches. Interestingly, defence lawyers were more likely to secure acquittal when they used vague and abstract language. Successful defence lawyers used measurably fewer adverbs than their less successful colleagues. Successful defence lawyers also used more legal jargon.

Parkinson and Parkinson (1979)

Evidence such as this suggests we should exercise caution in overstipulating particular word choices. Instead, you should be aware that different situations require different approaches, and make a conscious choice of speech tactics depending on your purpose.

There is no doubt that the choice of words affects an audience. In choosing words it is often important to select plain everyday words. Think about the way you speak and begin to form some good habits. Use only those words which you fully understand, choosing them carefully for your speeches to convey exactly the sentiment, fact or feeling which you intend. Remember that the active voice (for example, 'Jim Smith hit a fellow worker') is more vigorous than the passive (for example, 'Another worker was hit by Jim Smith'). As lawyers we tend to use neutral phraseology when we could be more positive. In an Industrial Tribunal, for example the respondent's advocate might say, 'The applicant's conduct in striking a fellow employee was gross misconduct fully warranting his dismissal'. This has less impact than 'Jim Smith was dismissed because he hit a fellow worker'.

Try to put important ideas at the beginning or end of the sentence. Compare:

'The defendant, at no stage, denied driving too fast'

And

'Not once has the defendant denied driving too fast'.

What is the important message and which sentence conveys it better?

Words should be chosen for particular purposes. Witness estimates of the speed of a motor vehicles can vary according to the verb used by the questioner to describe an accident. In American research into witnesses perception of a car crash, use of the word 'smashed' evoked an estimate of 40.8 mph, 'collided' 39.3 mph, 'bumped' 38.1 mph, 'hit' 34.0 mph and 'contacted' 31.8 mph. When the questioner used the word 'hit' witnesses were prepared to say that they had seen broken glass on the road. There was no broken glass. Asking 'did you see the car with **the** broken headlight' was more likely to get a 'Yes' than 'did you see the car with **a** broken headlight'. Therefore a plaintiff's advocate and a defendant's advocate would be wise to choose different words to describe the same accident.

Loftus (1974)

1.8 Words for impact

One reason for using short sentences is that they are more easily understood. Another is that they give longer sentences more force. Longer sentences can be made more attractive by a number of devices. Did you know, for example, that the interest of an audience is stimulated by a rhetorical question? I have noticed that, in skim reading a text, I often go back and reread a question if I have not fully grasped its meaning.

Using similies and metaphors is another way of stimulating interest in an audience and of increasing their understanding of your point. A good example is Pollock CB's observation that:

> *'It has been said that circumstantial evidence is to be considered as a chain, but that is not so, for then, if any one link broke, the chain would fall. It is more like the case of a rope comprised of several cards. One strand of the card might be insufficient to sustain the weight, but three stranded together may be of quite sufficient strength.'*

Exall (1966)
4 F&F 922

Another technique is the use of 'parallel phrases' (words or phrases in a sentence which echo other words or phrases in the sentence). John F Kennedy often used the rhythmic repetition of key words in his speeches, for example:

> *'Not merely peace in our time but peace for all time'.*

People notice and remember such phrases. For example in a recent murder trial a phrase widely quoted in the national press was:

> *'Nothing like his had ever happened before. Nothing like this has happened since'*

John Goldring QC
R v Allit

Churchill was fond of alliteration:

> *'We cannot fail or falter'* and *'He was a man of light and learning'.*

Another popular trick is to arrange points in groups of three. There is something about this number which is magical:-

> *'Research in conversation analysis, particularly by Jefferson, suggests that lists occurring in natural conversation are very*

frequently done in three parts. More important, three-partedness is a 'basic structural principle' to which speakers orient as a normative device, which is to say that lists with less than three items may be treated as incomplete ... This striking pervasiveness of three-parted patterns across kinds of discourse, and across cultures, is perhaps responsible for the research beginning to take place in the cognitive and linguistic sciences to look into the technical bases for three-part categorizations as ways of conceptually organising experience'.

Drew (1990)

'He was great; he was magic'

sounds like an excerpt from an interview with a footballer.

'He was great; he was magic; he was a star'

at least sounds like an excerpt from an interview with the manager. The sentence is balanced and the eulogy complete.

Theodore I Kossof (1977) gives an example of how 'parallel phrases' can be translated to legal contexts. Of his visit to the tomb of Napoleon Robert Ingersoll said:

'I saw him at Toulon, I saw him putting down the mob, I saw him at the head of an army, I saw him in Egypt, I saw him at Elba.'

He demonstrates how this might be adapted by an American trial lawyer in a child personal injury case:

'I saw this beautiful blonde haired child on her way to school. I saw her crossing the street. I saw her playing with her friends and laughing as they walked home ...'

While British courts may be used to less dramatic imagery the impact can be 'scaled down' to good effect. Do not aim to cram your presentation with verbal tricks; at the beginning you will have enough to cope with! Make sure that your delivery of that part which contains the key phrase is sufficiently emphasised by your pacing and often, a pause, usually immediately before delivery. Excessive repetition of any single device can lead your audience to see that it is just that; a device. If one comes to you in your preparation and it seems to serve a purpose, for example by making a key point memorable, then use it. Remember also that it is part of the art of presentation not just to use your phrase but to use it without a hint of either apology or embarrassment.

1.9 Emotion

Students often say that the quality they most appreciate in their lecturers is enthusiasm. Why should students be excited about a subject if their teacher isn't? It is the same for presentations of every kind. Why should a jury feel a sense of outrage if the prosecuting advocate can barely stifle a yawn? Why should they see this case as an instance of injustice when the defending advocate doesn't seem to care? Of course, emotion has to be kept in bounds. It needs to be channelled and controlled. But the court, just like an audience, should be in no doubt about your commitment to what you are doing.

> *'An advocate must be convincing, and for this purpose must himself be convinced of the merits of the points he is making. To put it bluntly he must look as if he believes every word of his client's instructions'.*
>
> Bartle(1983)

It is especially important that an advocate can portray a sincere conviction in her client's cause because she cannot *state* such a belief. The root of this convention is that it is not the advocate's role to express opinions in court. If both advocates said they believed their clients the argument could well be decided by the status or credibility of the advocate rather than by the evidence and the argument.

1.10 Repetition

There may be a very good reason for repeating a key point, for emphasis, for example. This is a variation of an old teaching adage 'tell them what you're going to tell them, tell them, and then tell them what you've told them'. Make sure that if you do repeat a point you vary the way in which you present it. Mere repetition is tedious. Having said that, there may be some occasions when you use exactly the same phrase again and again. This should be a conscious decision and not just the result of a failure of inspiration.

1.11   Pacing

Presenters often assume that the key to being understood is to speak slowly. In fact this is not the case. The human brain has the capacity to process information far more quickly than we can speak, provided it understands what is said. Presenters who speak too slowly can lose their audience to boredom. Provided attention is paid to the other key elements of presentation style a lively pace is necessary to keep the audience stimulated. Of course anxiety can lead to a rushed delivery but it is often not the pace which is the problem; it is the lack of variation in the voice and the lack of pauses which undermines delivery. Assume that you have something to say which deserves to be listened to; don't ever think 'let's get this over with and get out' or you will not do justice to yourself or your argument.

1.12   Pauses

Most speakers who are nervous do not speak too fast; their mistake is not to pause enough. When we get over-anxious time seems to speed up, and any delay seems like an age. The speaker is very conscious of pauses which are barely noticed by the audience. An audience needs pauses in order to process and organise information. Pauses can also be used tactically:

> 'Silence is one of the best ways to get attention. Suppose a lawyer is in the middle of a final argument and notices a juror in the back row whose eyes start to flutter closed. Does he raise his voice; change the subject; grab the jury rail and go on? No. He stops. Waits. Says nothing. The tension of the situation rises until

*all eyes are fixed on him unblinkingly. At that moment the lawyer
has the jury's total attention. The next thing he says or does will
be remembered ... It works so well the lawyer who uses it must
take special care that whatever follows justifies the expectation
which was created.'*

Kossof (1977)

1.13   Posture

Your posture helps to convey confidence; in addition, good
posture is an aid to voice projection and delivery. In some
situations you will stand. In others, particularly tribunals, you may
be invited to sit. If you are sitting, lean forwards rather than
backwards and do not cross your legs. When standing be upright
with your feet placed slightly apart and your weight evenly
distributed. Do not sway, either from side to side or backwards
and forwards. Hold any materials at a level which allows you to
conveniently maintain eye contact with your audience. Avoid
unnecessary movements with the hands. Finally, if it is possible
under the weight of all this advice, be relaxed; do not stand too
stiffly. Believe it or not, all of these things will help your voice as
well as looking better.

1.14   Interaction

One to one communication is usually the most effective means of
interaction:

Whatever the presentation it is important to interact with the
audience. When it is not possible to speak to the audience
individually the only means left is eye contact. Your eyes not only
hold the audience's attention. They tell you how the audience is
responding to what you are saying. Different people respond
differently to the same presentation. It is important to take cues
from the audience. If members of the jury are looking at the floor
or examining their fingernails perhaps your delivery needs more

pep. If the judge is clearly impatient, it may be appropriate for you to take the cue and respond by changing your presentation style, for example speeding up a little. It may be that you are covering aspects which she has gleaned from the papers (in which case she will usually say) or it may be that your delivery is too slow. However, some judges are just impatient. It may be that she has made up her mind about the case. If that is the situation as you read it, do not compromise. Make sure that what you have to say is heard.

1.15   Body language

There is evidence that non-verbal signals have more impact on an audience than either words or voice. We read these signals so automatically we rarely consciously analyse them. Furthermore, there is a danger in trying to change signals:

> *'Human beings cannot function with equanimity when too much detail is brought to the level of awareness. Blind spots are a protection in a sense. Bringing too much to the attention of a person, about the way she fiddles with her hands, or grimaces, or uses over-high pitch too often, will not enhance communication, and may push the individual to isolation.'*
>
> Key (1975)

If there is little you can do to change your own body language what is the point of knowing about non-verbal communication? Firstly, of course, be conscious of other people's signals. If you observe you will know whether or not the audience is with you. As to your own body language obviously you should try and avoid the most distracting of your mannerisms. The most important point is not to send verbal messages which are inconsistent with your non-verbal messages; you must be sure that the words you use are consistent with your feelings. The problem in denying your feelings in presentation is that an audience perceives your lack of conviction or belief.

In advocacy you are always more likely to be convincing if you believe in what you are saying.

> *'I am very much impressed with the work of men like Professor Ray Birdwhistle, who insists that more than 50% of all communication between human beings is being done non-verbally - that is by eyebrows, ears, shoulders, set, movement, tone. His observations are true; a lawyer cannot fake his way through a case and con a jury into a verdict he does not believe in himself. The jurors will know they are being conned; they will resent being thought of as such easy marks'*

> Spangenburg (1977)

According to Stefano (1977), this is an argument for honesty. If your client is an unsympathetic character it may be that you will be more convincing once you have confronted that problem. How? You can admit it; having done so you may be more able to put his case convincingly. That is a position which you can believe in. If you believe in what you are doing your body and voice are more likely to act in concert; you will be persuasive.

On body language generally, see also 'Negotiation' by Diana Tribe and 'Interviewing & Counselling' by Jenny Chapman, both in this series. On reading the body language of your audience, see Exercise One later in this Chapter.

1.16   Appearance

An advocate owes a client a duty to do the best she can. Whatever your personal preferences in clothes they may not be the judge's.

> *'Personal impression of the advocate inevitably influences a court either favourably or adversely ... A dark suit and sober tie is the ideal working uniform of the lawyer. If a waistcoat is not worn the jacket should be buttoned up. A degree of individuality there must be but these are surely sound guidelines'*

> Bartle (1983)

While much depends on the person who hears the case you will rarely know what they think of your striking apparel, or how they are influenced by your appearance. Why make a sartorial point at your client's expense? Be yourself, but less so, is good advice. Looking right helps you to feel right: feeling right gives you confidence.

1.17   Confidence and nerves

Stumbling nervousness focuses attention on you rather than your case. It is a disadvantage but one which can be dealt with. There are possibly worse personality traits; pomposity and arrogance may give an audience an unhealthy desire to see you take a fall. Some people appear naturally confident about speaking in public. Others can be badly affected by nerves. You can't worry and think at the same time.

Confidence grows with experience of the context in which you are operating, realising that you can do it. Have as many 'good experiences' early on as you can get; you could probably do ten or more simulated presentations of a particular type before you will feel confident. You can usually tell you are confident when you start to feel bored! The best way to ensure good experiences is to prepare well. This includes not just the substantive law and arguments but the procedure as well. If the procedure requires that you make an opening address, think carefully about what you will say and rehearse those opening lines so that you can deliver them with confidence. Do not read them out loud; you will appear and feel less confident. **Do not** take a lack of positive signals from the audience as a judgement on you; assume the audience's acceptance. Finally, focus clearly on the task before you, how you are going to solve this problem. Do not think about what others may be thinking of you.

Nerves are natural before a 'performance'. Usually, they disappear as you continue. The trick is to get over the early stages. If you find yourself badly affected it is a good idea, if possible, to make physical contact with some object. Sit down, hold the edge of the desk or hold your hands behind your back; this will prevent your hands shaking. Focus on what is going on and wait for the moment to pass. When you think about the performance imagine it going really well; positive thinking is a great aid to confidence.

1.18   Elements of competent performance

There are many ways of analysing presentation and breaking down the skills involved. In fact these skills are largely interconnected. If you are confident and have good posture there is a good chance you will better control of your voice, pacing and the interaction in general.

Key work on the nature of lawyer competence was conducted by The Competency-Based Task Force of the Antioch School of Law published in 1978. The Task Force identified six 'major competencies'. One of these major competencies, oral competency, they broke these down into seven 'competencies':

'1) ability to use the mechanics of language (eg grammar,syntax, articulation

2) ability to express a thought with preciseness, clarity and economy

3) ability to express thoughts in an organised manner

4) ability to speak appropriately to a given audience

5) ability to identify and use appropriate non-verbal aspects of communications (eg appearance, poise, gestures, facial expressions, posture and use of spatial relationships)

6) ability to perceive other's communications and actions (verbal and non-verbal)

7) ability to communicate so as to advance immediate and long-term objectives'

Checklists such as this one can be useful guides and can help to identify major shortcomings or provide a structure for verbal feedback in small group work. Being aware of a shortcoming is initially discomfiting. It is also the first step in remedying that shortcoming. If you need to improve your basic presentation take every opportunity to do so; speak in public whenever you can and invite feedback from any audience prepared to give it. Do not become obsessed with how you are perceived by others. It is difficult to significantly change the way you are. With effort you might avoid a few annoying mannerisms or appreciate that you could be more or less assertive. If you try and change **too** much you can become over anxious, self conscious and, as a result, less effective. In most cases time and experience will improve performance.

Exercise One

Try this with a few friends for a start.

Select a topic of particular interest to you, a hobby or current issue, for example. Talk for five to ten minutes each to an audience of four or five colleagues about your chosen topic. At the end of the presentation the audience should give you constructive feedback identifying particular strengths and weaknesses of the presentation based on the Antioch criteria listed above. In particular, consider the following points:

(i) look back at criterion seven (advancing immediate and long-term objectives). Consider the purpose of your presentation. Is it to inform, persuade or sell? How should you introduce this purpose? How will you structure what you say to achieve it?

(ii) re-read criteria five and six (using non-verbal communication and perceiving others' (non-verbal) communications or actions). Remember that it is difficult to do either of these things effectively if you are looking down reading notes; you need to be able to scan the faces of the audience to see what signals they are sending you. The benefit of this kind of exercise is that it gives you experience of working from brief notes or headings. It can be an essential confidence builder and should not be treated lightly. In seeking honest feedback from your audience try and recall the signals you received from individuals in the audience. Test whether you understood the non-verbal messages they sent. You can do this by asking each individual what they were feeling at the time they did whatever they did:

Q: 'Jim, I noticed you folded your arms when I was talking about abortion. What were you feeling?

A: Actually I was feeling cold and thought I might disrupt your talk if I put my jacket on.

Q: Are you sure? It felt like a defensive gesture to me.

A: Well, I didn't agree with what you were saying but I wasn't aware of shutting it out'.

It's often the case that non-verbal messages are ambiguous or misunderstood. The fact that non-verbal signals from an audience can be ambiguous is worth noting. However, 'body language' can be a powerful tool in communication and it is surprising, therefore, that some students appear reluctant to take the subject of non-verbal communication seriously. Positive body language can be an aid to effective advocacy. The sooner you start thinking about it, and finding a language which will express your thoughts, the sooner you can begin to improve your presentation.

The first time you try the exercise the audience should not interrupt. If you want a second round, pick a controversial current issue. A further refinement is to allow questions during the presentation. The presenter can then practice dealing with difficult questions. They might, for example, respond to questions as asked or deflect them. You will soon develop strategies for deflecting even the most disruptive contribution from the floor. For example:

Speaker: Next, I am going to talk about the current rash of cases involving corruption in the boardrooms of our major companies ...

Questioner: (not sure whether to take this seriously): What about
             the workers?

Speaker: You may be right; worker democracy is a possible
             solution. I will consider this, and some other options,
             in my concluding remarks.

1.19 Narrative

The average attention span of most people is no more than 10 to
12 minutes. After that time our thoughts wander and may only be
brought back by a presenter using a technique like audience
participation, silence or questions. A possible exception to this is
when we are listening to an story with real human interest. If our
interest is stimulated in this way our attention is stimulated, we
want more detail; we want to find out what happens to the
characters we have identified with.

Narrative is no more or less than telling a story. Creating 'word
pictures' can be of great assistance in presenting a case to a
court. It can offer members of a jury a clear image of events.
Remember that they will know nothing about the case and it is
difficult for them to understand the story when they cannot easily
ask questions. Of course, to have the dynamic interest of a real
story they will need to identify with the characters and care about
what happens to them; the characters will have to be real and the
world which they inhabit will have to be clearly drawn. Of course,
in courts of law 'the story' has to be accurate. This is not a
problem. It is not legal cases which are lacking in drama; it is the
way in which we analyse and report cases which tends to remove
the human interest. An advocate has to find the human dimension
of a story before he can turn the facts of a case into narrative.

Many of the techniques which can be used in developing
narrative come from the best dramatic traditions. Konstantin
Stanislavsky originated 'the method' school of acting at the and of
the last century. His aim was to eliminate the artificiality of the
acting of the period. His approach was to develop the 'emotional

memory' of actors in their roles. In modern acting this is known as 'imaging'. Heightened perception of events is achieved by focusing on a character and a situation. The events are mentally reconstructed in minute detail using a sensory checklist; sight, hearing, touch, smell, taste and state of mind.

According to Kerper (1984), the technique is useful in creating a heightened perception of a series of events. It is useful preparation for interviewing the client prior to litigation and for questioning witnesses in court. A sense of narrative can be an important aid in making speeches and cross-examining witnesses.

It is worth repeating that, in using any of the devices mentioned above, you must be aware of your audience; their needs, their expectations and, possibly, their prejudices. Do not use presentation techniques you are not comfortable with. Avoid any hint that you may be patronising your audience or attempting to manipulate them.

Exercise Two

In order to develop your sense of narrative take a case which is well known to you. *Donoghue v Stevenson* or *Carlill v Carbolic Smokeball* or the *Wagonmound* are usually lodged in most students' memories. For the purpose of demonstration I will take the Wagonmound. You will remember that the fire which damaged Sheerlegs wharf, and the ships moored there, followed the spillage of oil into Sydney harbour at Caltex wharf. You might start by making a mind map of the basic facts of the case as a guide. You will need to identify the characters; the ship's engineer, the welders and their works manager and the 'higher authority' he consulted before instructing the men to continue their welding operation.

Case reports offer scant detail of the basic facts and, for the purpose of this exercise, they are not really important. The questions which you might have asked the characters are for you to answer; the idea is to free your imagination. You can approach the task from the partisan perspective of any of the characters or none. However, a perspective that you might like to adopt is one which suggests this is an event which was unforeseeable, not in a legal sense, but to the ordinary people who were involved at the time. The first time you do this its best just to concentrate on the story. The idea is to make a story come alive. The story can be recounted seriously or with humour as you prefer; some people feel more comfortable with humour to start with. Since this is not an exercise in factual or legal accuracy I will dispense with both.

The sun beat down on Sydney Harbour and the quayside and wharves hummed with the activity of people and insects. Along at Sheerlegs wharf Ron Welder ignored the heat and the stale smell of sweat and solder. He exhaled noisily as the flame of his oxy-acetylene torch burst into noisy action. HMS Doomed would need all of Ron's skills to save its rust flecked carcass. Ron was an experienced man, a man of 35 years who loved welding; his father had been a welder and Ron had been apprenticed to a welder from the age of 16. He had learned his trade so well that when, at the age of 21, he had wanted to marry Arlene there was money enough to support them; Ron's overtime had seen to that.

That morning the work had seemed unusually slow; the air was still and damp. Many of the male welders had taken off their shirts. At around noon Ron and his mates were enjoying thick sandwiches and a tin of piping hot, sweet tea. Leaning on the rail of HMS Doomed, Ron sucked on a can of beer. 'Looks like an oil spill out there' he heard someone on the upper deck call. The gang gathered round and shielded their eyes against the sun. They saw a patch of dark sea moving slowly but surely towards Sheerlegs. Ron wondered whether the welding would be affected. He knew that his overtime was at risk from the gathering gloom in the water. With his overtime might go his planned trip to England to see his mum and dad. As Ron had kissed Arlene goodbye that morning he could not have guessed that his would be the spark that ignited global litigation. Ron's torch would be the catalyst in a chain of events which established a startling new test for the limit of legal responsibility for negligent conduct.

But it was not Ron whose conduct on that day was condemned as negligent. The SS Wagonmound had put into Sydney Harbour to collect a cargo of bunkering oil. It was about 10 am. On deck the engineer, Dave Sloppy was supervising the pumping of oil into the hold ...

This would be a good point for you to take over! In about three pages you should get to the interesting bit; the decision to carry on welding, the spark falling in the cotton waste floating in the water and the fire which followed. Remember to subject each item on your mind map to the sensory checklist (see above) in order to develop the narrative. You should be able to expand the detailed description to fill the time allowed to you.

1.20 Summary

- Persuasion has an emotional and logical dimension
- Anticipate the needs of your audience
- Start and finish strongly
- Use creativity in planning
- Speak at a normal pace using pauses and eye contact
- Give your words and phrases impact, but....
- Do not be seen to manipulate your audience
- Believe your message
- Develop confidence through trial runs
- Be conscious of your 'story line

1.21 End of chapter references and additional reading

Bartle R A
(1983)
Advocacy in the Magistrates Court
Law Institute Journal Vol 57

Drew P
(1990)
Language in the Judicial Process
Plenum Press

Du Cann R
(1980)
The Art of the Advocate
Penguin

Evans K
(1992)
Advocacy at the Bar:
A Beginner's Guide
Ch 16
Blackstone Press

Gelb M
(1988)
Present Yourself
Aurum Press

Guirdham M and
Tyler K
(1992)
Enterprise Skills for Students
Ch 8
Butterworth Heinemann

Kerper J
(1984)
Staninslavsky in the Courtroom
Litigation Vol 10 No 4

Key M R
(1975)
Paralanguage and Kinesics
Scarecrow

King A G
(1992)
Effective Communication
Ch 4
Blackstone Press

Kossof T I
(1977)
The Language of Persuasion
Litigation Vol 3 No 4

Loftus E
(1974)
Reconstructing Memory:
The Incredible Witness
Psychology Today Vol 1

Parkinson M G and
Parkinson L M
(1979)
*Speech Tactics for
Successful Trials*
Trial Vol 15 No 9

Rifkind S H
(1984)
How to Try a Non-Jury
Litigation Vol 10 No 3

Spangenburg C
(1977)
*Basic Values and the
Techniques of Persuasion*
Litigation Vol 3 No 4

Stephano J
(1977)
Body Language and Persuasion
Litigation Vol 5 No 4 1

Vinson D E
(1985)
How to Persuade Jurors
American Bar Association
Journal Vol 71

CHAPTER

2 Conduct

The ethical conduct of solicitors is governed by principles established by the Law Society and published in 'The Guide to the Professional Conduct of Solicitors'. Some of the principles bear specifically on solicitors acting as advocates. Others are relevant in less obvious ways. There are additional conventions which should be followed. These often arise out of an obligation of common courtesy to the court.

2.1 The lawyer and the client

Many clients today want to be closely involved in their case; they want to know what is happening and to participate fully in the decisions which are made. They want to know what they are 'buying' and they no longer work from an assumption that their lawyer is competent.

> 'Today it is necessary to give your client more information than before. There is more pressure to inform and the character of modern litigation is more complex ... we have to be careful about what we say and how we say it; to be knowledgeable about procedures, costs and the consequences of litigation...'
>
> Boon (1992)

The client will often expect the lawyer/client relationship to be more of a partnership than in former years. This is a perfectly reasonable expectation. Often the client is running a considerable financial risk in litigation. The lawyer cannot guarantee that the case will be won. The client is aware that the outcome may depend on what the lawyer puts into the case so you can be sure that the client wants to know what is going on! Potential problems can be eased if the lawyer recognises this legitimate interest and involves the client as far as possible, keeping him informed of developments, re-evaluating the possible outcome and guiding the client in making decisions (see 'Client Case: A Guide for Solicitors' The Law Society (1991) especially pp 10 & 11).

Principles 14.14 and 14.15 of the 'Guide to the Professional Conduct of Solicitors' impose an obligation on a solicitor appearing for the defence in criminal cases or in civil proceedings to 'say on behalf of the client what the client should properly say for himself if he possessed the requisite skill and knowledge'.

This means that you must first discover what the client 'should properly say for himself'. It implies proper counselling of the client to determine the client's objectives and interests in order that you are able to adequately advise on options and obtain proper instructions.

In matters of all kinds the advocate must discover all the facts from the client. She will sometimes need to work hard to create an atmosphere of openness and trust. It may be necessary to explain the duty of confidentiality in order to obtain all the available information. It is only possible to advise properly on the basis of the full facts and this should be made clear to the client. A client should be fully aware of the risks he or she runs if he or she does not provide you with all the information you require. One such risk is that the information will come out at trial and torpedo their case. This could leave them with a burden of ruinous costs in a civil case or a more onerous sentence than necessary in a criminal case. However, having obtained this information you can only give the client preliminary advice on the basis of what you have been told. Your view of the matter may change when you have heard what the other side have to say. At that point you may wish to go back to your client and discuss the matter further.

'I am accustomed also to plead to him the cause of his adversary, in order to engage him to plead his own, and to state boldly what he thinks of his own case. When he is gone I conceive myself in three characters, my own, that of my adversary and that of the judge. Whatever circumstance is such as to promise more support or assistance than obstruction I resolve to speak up on it;

wherever I find more harm than good, I set aside and totally reject that part'.

Cicero 'De Oratore'

Cicero's advice is still relevant to client interviews. In a recent research project a solicitor explained how she adopted the role of the trial judge in advising a client:

'When dealing with a client it is important to put a neutral cap on and remain objective. In other words put yourself in the place of the trial judge ... it is important also to be brave with the client - let them know from the start what the likelihood of success or failure is - don't raise their hopes if they have little chance of success'.

Another solicitor anticipated the line which would be taken by the other side:

'I attempt to remain objective by placing myself in the other solicitor's shoes and try to explain this to the client who can then sometimes see things in a different light ...'

Boon (1992)

The foundation of effective advocacy, therefore, is getting litigation off on the right course; this requires that you obtain the full facts in as accurate a form as possible. How do you obtain full disclosure by the client? It would be foolish to tell the client in advance that you do not wish to hear admissions or details of incriminating evidence. However, this presents problems. Principle 14.08 of 'The Guide to the Professional Conduct of Solicitors' states that if a client informs a solicitor that they have committed perjury or misled the court on a material point the solicitor must decline to act further unless the client agrees that the conduct is disclosed in full.

The ethical dilemma of many lawyers is more complex than a quick reading of this principle suggests. First of all the client must inform the solicitor that they have committed perjury. What is a material point? What if the client says he is going to commit perjury in the future? What if the perjury is obvious to the solicitor but is not admitted? Canadian research suggests that the huge majority of advocates put their obligations to clients before their obligations to the court.

The court must rely on the good sense of advocates in such matters. After all, if a client is determined to mislead the court they can go to another advocate. This time they will omit the detail which caused the first to withdraw. Protected by the first advocate's duty of confidentiality they will lie to the court and may or may not be believed.

Clearly then, it is the advocate's duty to convince the client that it is too risky to lie. If they have a good case without lying this is an argument which can be pressed. To be found lying to the court on one issue will undermine the client's credibility on other issues. If they have no case without lying the risk of being caught out is too risky; there are other options, such as negotiation, which should be urged on the client.

The lawyer's duty to her client also extends to adequately preparing him for a court performance.

Research conducted in the United States indicates that, in criminal trials, defendants are more likely to be acquitted if they:

i)   said 'please' or 'sir' when appropriate

ii) spoke in grammatically complete sentences

iii) made fewer references to themselves.

2.2   The lawyer and the court

Principle 14.13 of 'The Guide' provides that a solicitor prosecuting a criminal case must make every material point supporting the prosecution but that 'in presenting the evidence must do so dispassionately and with scrupulous fairness'. Thus, details of witnesses whose testimony favours the accused should be disclosed to the defence. There is no corresponding duty on the defence.

The advocate must show all due respect to the court and is entitled to be shown courtesy by the officials of the court. The materials from the Inns of Court School of Law Bar Finals course give extensive examples. The conventions for addressing the official in charge of the hearing are summarised here. You should avoid referring to the senior court official as 'You', as in:

'You will see that the defendant has a long record.'

The forms which are used to avoid this seem strange at first but you will soon become accustomed to them. They can be summarised as follows:

Magistrates, Tribunal Chairs and District Judges are addressed as 'Sir' or 'Madam'. On occasions where there are other members of the bench or tribunal, address the Chair and refer to these others as 'colleagues', for example:

'Madam, the applicant and respondents have agreed terms'.

'If it pleases you Sir, I have copies for your colleagues.'

County Court judges and Circuit Judges sitting in the Crown Court are addressed as 'Your Honour', for example:

'If Your Honour could turn to page 15 of the Plaintiff's bundle'. 'His Honour will direct you on the law at the end of the trial.'

High Court Judges, Appeal Court Judges and people sitting as judges in the Central Criminal Court are addressed 'My Lord' or 'My Lady' in any situation where you might use the judge's name, for example:

'Please show My Lord the scar.'

Use 'My Lordship' or 'My Ladyship' in situations where you otherwise use 'you', for example:

'Does Your Ladyship wish that this witness be released?'

Magistrate's clerks are referred to as 'your learned clerk' when addressing the bench.

As regards other advocates, only barristers refer to each other as 'my learned friend'. Solicitors refer to each other by name.

There is obviously more to the relationship between advocates and judges than terms of address with feudal undertones; these are simply manifestations of a deeper obligation. Both judges and lawyers have reciprocal obligations to uphold the dignity of the courts of justice. This is eloquently expressed in the Code of Trial Conduct of the American College of Trial Lawyers:

> 'During the trial a lawyer should always display a courteous, dignified and respectful attitude towards the judge presiding, not for the sake of his person, but for the maintenance of respect for and confidence in the judicial office. The judge, to render effective such conduct, has reciprocal responsibilities of courtesy to and respect for the lawyer who is also an officer of the court. It is both the right and duty of a lawyer fully and properly to present his client's cause, to insist on the opportunity to do so, and further, to take appropriate steps to attempt to assure that his client is granted a fair and impartial trial. He should vigorously present all proper arguments against rulings or court demeanour he deems erroneous or prejudicial, and see to it that an accurate and complete case record is made. In any regard he should not be deterred by any fear of judicial displeasure or punishment'.

> Connolly (1975)

It is important therefore to be respectful to the court. This includes avoiding the use of the time honoured phrase 'with respect'. This phrase is common amongst lawyers, particularly at the point when the advocate is about to disagree with a point. However, it is generally recognised that 'respect' is probably the last thing conveyed by its use.

2.3   Conflicts

On occasions the advocate's duty to the court and her duty to her client will conflict. This is an area in which there will often be disagreement amongst senior practitioners about what a lawyer should do when faced with such a conflict. Principle 14.01 of the Guide provides that:

'a solicitor who acts in litigation, whilst owing a duty to his client to do his best for him, must never deceive or mislead the court.'

Thus, a solicitor who realises that another advocate has missed a case or provision must draw this to the attention of the court, even if it may damage her own case.

Under Principle 14.02 a solicitor must not

'make an allegation which is intended only to insult, degrade or annoy the other side, the witness or any other person.'

This precludes impugning parties who are not party to the proceedings before the court or making allegations against witnesses which are not supported on reasonable grounds.

Apart from certain conduct which is specifically precluded by the rules:

'It is for all participants to extend respect and courtesy and to expect to receive it. The most visible sign of shared respect is appropriate courtroom demeanour and manners.'

This actually serves the best interest of both advocate and client because:

'If counsel is a bully, a braggart, a boor it is best to assume a more amenable personality ... Juries come to their duties with their own common sense and life experience, which the judge usually tells them they are to use in deciding the case. This common experience includes the ability to spot someone who is posturing, declaiming, faking or otherwise trying to baffle them with form over substance.'

Steingrass (1985)

2.4   Lawyers and witnesses

Much of what is said in this section is as applicable to client witnesses as to other witnesses of fact. In interviewing witnesses before trial it is important to make it clear that their evidence may be disregarded or diminished in value if it is perceived to be partial. A witness whose evidence may otherwise be valuable may destroy a whole case if they are not believed on what may appear to be a trivial detail. There are therefore tactical as well as ethical issues in ensuring that witnesses provide a full and an accurate proof of evidence. There are particular problems in assessing 'vulnerable' witnesses.

> 'Falsification or distortion of memory is particularly pronounced where an individual reflects an acute sense of insecurity and an immature outlook on life. Fabrications reflect an attempt to achieve status and recognition, and to dispel any doubts as to one's efficiency'.
>
> Freedman (1976)

However, there are other factors which lead different witnesses to give different accounts of the same events; the very act of recounting a personal experience, and the questions which prompt recollection, can affect the detail of what witnesses offer as fact.

> 'One of the most common misconceptions about memory is that it is a process of recollection or reproduction of impressions, closely analogous to the functioning of a phonograph or tape recorder. In that respect legal thinking is centuries out of date, proceeding as if highly relevant experiments in behavioural psychology had never taken place. In fact perceiving is itself active and constructive and memory is much more a process of reconstruction than one of recollection or recall. Moreover, the process is a highly creative one, affecting what is 'remembered' as much as what is 'forgotten''!
>
> Freedman (1976)

Closed and leading questions in interviewing are more likely to shape the witnesses recollection of events (on questioning strategies in client interviews generally see also 'Interviewing & Counselling' by Jenny Chapman in this series). Adversarial court procedure often gives each side exclusive access to some witnesses. There is a risk in this situation that the witnesses for each side will have their evidence 'shaped' during trial preparation. When they give their evidence they will not be lying. That is the way they now remember events. Recognising this also involves recognising the thin ethical line between obtaining a witness' account of events and determining what they will say about the events.

For this reason cross-examination of witnesses is not always effective in obtaining 'the truth'. Cross-examination may not secure the best account of events; the hope is that from all the evidence produced at a trial a synthesis will produce something which better equates with historical accuracy.

'Narrative supplemented by probing questions of the direct examination type have been found to induce the least error and cover the most ground, ie in obtaining a complete story of what was in fact observed, whereas the experimental findings illustrate that highly suggestive or leading questions usually associated with cross-examination cause a witness to give answers which are very high in the percentage of error'.

Grossman (1962)

It may be obvious at the time you speak to a witness that he has given information which conflicts with other known facts. On other occasions matters come to light which contradict what the witness has said. On these occasions it is important to speak to the witness face to face. It is difficult to clarify even a simple point on the telephone or to convey to a witness the importance of their credibility.

It is also important to realise that witnesses who are contradicted are not necessarily lying; they should not be treated as if they are. In speaking to your witness it is more likely that you will get an accurate version of what they know if you question on the basis that they may be mistaken. You might suggest to the witness that the other side might try to show that he is lying but that is another matter. Witnesses in court are also entitled to common courtesy. It is not good tactics to attack every witness as if they must be lying unless, of course, you can quite clearly show that they are.

> *'Aggressiveness towards witnesses or discourtesy to the bench is always counter-productive ... He who seeks to persuade the court to look favourably on his client will not achieve this objective by antagonising his audience'.*

> Bartle (1983)

In questioning a witness you should not ask a trick question, for example, one which misrepresents a state of affairs or what another witness has said. In any closing speech reviewing the evidence you should not misquote the evidence of a witness.

What is the situation if you suspect one of your own witnesses of perjury? Is the client to be denounced because a witness has lied on their behalf? The Guide is not clear on this point although the general prohibition on misleading the court presumably applies (see above). Probably the strict ethical position is that an advocate should not ask questions which she knows will allow a witness to give false evidence. Nor should she refer to evidence she knows to be false in a closing speech. However, as we have seen, the boundary between what is 'true' and 'false' is rarely clearly defined; you may find that different advocates may have different views about whether a witness has given 'false' evidence.

2.5   Summary

- Treat all participants in the court process with respect

- Use correct terms of address

- Your duty to your client is subordinate to your duty to the court

- Be brave in confronting your client with problems in the case

- Be brave in presenting your clients' case

- Expose inconsistencies in your witness' story before you get to court

- Counsel your witnesses against perjury and disqualify yourself if necessary

2.6   End of chapter references and additional reading

Bartle R A   *Advocacy in the Magistrates Court*
(1983)   Law Institute Journal Vol 57

Bing I   *Criminal Procedure & Sentencing*
(1992)   *in the Magistrate's Court*
                         Ch 11
                         Sweet & Maxwell

Boon A   *Skills for legal functions I:*
(1992)   *Representation and Advice*
                         Institute of Advanced Legal Studies

Boon A   *Assessing Competence to Conduct*
(1992)   *Civil Litigation Key Tasks and Skills*
                         Institute of Advanced Legal Studies

Carey Miller D L   *The Advocate's Duty to Justice:*
(1981)   *Where Does it Belong?*
                         Law Quarterly Review Vol 97

Connolly P R   *Civility in the Courtroom: The*
(1975)   *Judge's Obligation*
                         Litigation Vol 1 No 1

Du Cann R   *The Art of the Advocate*
(1980)   Ch 2
                         Penguin Books

Duggan M and   *Material non-disclosure on ex parte*
Gott I   *applications - The Golden Rule: Part I*
(1986-7)   Litigation Vol 6

Freedman M H   *Counselling the Client: Refreshing*
(1976)   *Recollection or Prompting Perjury?*
                         Litigation Vol 2 No 3

Grossman B A (1962)	*Testing Witness Reliability* Criminal Law Quarterly Vol 5
Inns of Court School of Law (1992)	*Advocacy, Negotiation and Conference skills* Blackstone Press
Napley D (1991)	*The Technique of Persuasion* Ch 2 Sweet & Maxwell
Steingrass S (1985)	*A Judge's 10 Tips on Courtroom Success* American Bar Association Journal Vol 71
Silverman F (1992)	*Handbook of Professional Conduct for Solicitors* Butterworths
The Law Society (1990)	*Guide to the Professional Conduct of Solicitors* The Law Society
The Law Society (1991)	*A Guide for Solicitors* The Law Society
The Law Society (1991)	*Client Care: A Guide for Solicitors* The Law Society
Thomas A P (1986-7)	*The Solicitor and the Witness* Litigation 271

CHAPTER

3 Planning

> '... Diligence, I say, which as it avails in all things, is also
> of the utmost importance in pleading causes. Diligence is
> to be particularly cultivated by us; it is to be constantly
> exerted; it is capable of affecting almost everything ...'
>
> Cicero 'De Oratore'

3.1 The client

In any litigation you may handle the client is a valuable resource. They will usually have at their fingertips most of the factual information necessary for the preparation of their case. For this reason, interviewing techniques which increase the amount of detail are recommended.

The type of questions asked are important. The main distinctions are between open (or open ended), probing and closed questions. Open questions permit the client to talk at length; for example, 'Can you tell me about your background?' Probing questions supplement open questions and encourage elaboration of the account; for example, is 'can you tell me more about that?'. Closed questions require a very short answer; for example, is 'where were you born?'

Open questions supplemented by probing questions are a good foundation. They get the information and encourage the client to tell their own story. Probing questions encourage the client to see that detail is important; they keep up the flow of information. They may supplement open questions, as above, or, by using the sensory checklist, can stimulate recollection of the small, apparently insignificant details of key incidents. Closed questions can be used to clarify detail or in recapping on parts of the story. You might say, for example, 'so, if I can summarise what you have told me, you were not at the Purple Parrot when the crime was committed but you were at The Goose and Turkey which is five streets away, is that right?' (See also 'Interviewing & Counselling' by Jenny Chapman in this series.)

The client's value as a source of information may go beyond their knowledge of factual matters. In many civil cases expert opinion may be crucial. The commercial client may have come across well respected professionals in their own sphere of business, eg accountants, engineers or surveyors who may be prepared to give evidence; the personal injury victim will have views on the consultants he has seen, including they might make good expert witnesses; another client may have contacts with campaigning organisations who know of suitable experts.

At the end of the investigation phase the client expects clear advice about the prospects of success. It has long been recognised that the 'facts' which determine the outcome of cases are not necessarily 'historically accurate'. Jerome Frank, writing in 1949, answered his own question 'Is the finding of fact in a case what actually happened?'

> *'Most emphatically not. At best, it is only what the trial court, the trial judge or jury, thinks happened. What the trial court thinks happened may, however, be hopelessly incorrect. But that does not matter-legally speaking. For court purposes, what the court thinks about the facts is all that matters'.*

> Frank (1949)

Because cases depend on findings of fact the advocate should always be cautious in predicting the outcome of a trial; there is no such thing as a certain outcome. It follows that it is the rare case which will come to trial. In some areas of litigation, personal injury for example, most specialist practitioners bring less than 5% of their cases to trial. One of the prime rules of litigation is to proceed expeditiously but to be aware of opportunities for settlement.

3.2   Planning contexts

If you handle a case from the stage of the initial interview you will
be familiar with the issues and materials. On other occasions you
may be expected to speak on behalf of a client you have not met.
In these circumstances you may be handed a bundle of
documents generated by someone else.

In either case your preparation for advocacy should include a
thorough review of the case papers. The sequence in which you
go through the preparatory steps may vary depending on the
circumstances and the context. Generally, however, your first step
in preparing for advocacy, whether in the civil or the criminal
courts, will be to ask 'what are the contentious issues in this
case?'

3.2.1   Civil cases

Disputed facts should be evident from the pleadings in civil cases.
The system of pleading is designed explicitly to isolate the
matters in issue for the benefit of the parties and the court.
However, it is a feature of the common law that a defendant can
rely on alternative defences. Thus

> *'Irving Younger says that, at common law, you are allowed to*
> *reply to the plaintiff who claims his cabbages were eaten by your*
> *goat:*
>
> *You did not have any cabbages*
>
> *If you did, they were not eaten*
>
> *If they were eaten, it was not by a goat*
>
> *If they were eaten by a goat it was not my goat*
>
> *And if it was my goat, he was insane'*

McElhaney (1979)

If the pleadings fail to reveal the bone of contention, it may
become clear in a number of other ways. It may be necessary to

serve formal documents seeking clarification; a Request for Further and Better Particulars of a pleading, or interrogatories. In other cases less formal means may help to identify issues. The exchange of correspondence or the process of negotiation (see also 'Negotiation' by Diana Tribe in this series).

It is always advisable to gain as much knowledge as possible about the other side's case. Sometimes pleadings raise many issues such as where the plaintiff cites several allegations in the Statement of Claim. Notices to admit facts or documents may further limit the issues to be tried. From 16 November 1992 the parties in High Court and County Court actions will disclose the statements of those witnesses of fact on whom they intend to rely at trial. The periods for exchange are 14 weeks from close of pleadings in the High Court and 10 weeks in the County Court: Rules of the Supreme Court (Amendment No 2) 1992 (S1 1992 No 1907), County Court (Amendment No 2) Rules 1992. (S1 1992 No 1965). The application of these new rules may be varied by order of the court. It is already the case that expert reports were exchanged before trial. The advocate must be prepared to deal with all those matters which appear to be in dispute when the case is tried.

3.2.2   Criminal cases

In criminal cases the issues are usually issues of fact. The prosecutor has to prove the commission of the offence and that the accused committed it. The defence can choose which limb of the prosecutor's burden to challenge; what Marcus Stone calls the 'rule of alternative defence'. Typically the selection of one issue by the defence excludes the possibility of running the other. This follows because, if the defendant says he was not there, he cannot deny that a crime was committed. A defendant who denies that a crime was committed places himself in the position that he cannot deny his presence. Usually, it is only the defence advocate who will know which of these 'alternatives' will constitute the defence.

The prosecution may discover details of the defence either informally or through committal proceedings. In some cases the precise nature of the defence will only become clear as the defence evidence is presented during the trial itself. However, it is often possible to anticipate the likely issues at trial from the kind of offence charged. Stone suggests that there are three distinct types of crime:

- crimes which produce specific results (for example murder)
- crimes which are based on conduct rather than a result (for example assault)
- crimes which arise because of the accused's relationship to forbidden objects (for example possession of drugs)

In the vast majority of cases the critical issues for the defence will be similar. So, for result crimes, the potential issues may range from identification to intention. The prosecution is not necessarily hindered by not knowing precise details of the defence because the range of possible defences is limited. The prosecutor will wish to paint a full picture of the circumstances and to prove each element of the offence charged in any case. The defence is entitled to argue, at the end of the prosecution case, that the prosecutor has failed to do this and that the case should be dismissed. However, anticipating the common patterns of defence enables the prosecutor to plan and structure the case. (See Stone (1988))

3.3 Planning to use witness evidence

Witness evidence is divided into evidence of fact and opinion evidence. 'Fact' witnesses are not supposed to express opinions. Opinions can be expressed by suitably qualified experts. Experts are frequently asked to examine the scene of an accident or physical evidence. They will write a report which sets out the factual background and their opinion based on the evidence to hand. In magistrates' courts expert opinion is often given in statements which are accepted by both sides. In civil cases, and in the Crown Court, expert evidence is often challenged and experts are therefore required to justify their opinion in court.

3.3.1   Witnesses of fact

Most court cases involve factual disputes. Cautious lawyers treat their client's version of the facts with suspicion. The client may not wish to reveal elements of their story which may affect the lawyer's view of them or their case. In these instances the client seems to believe that their task is to convince their own lawyer of the merits of their case rather than the court. It is important, therefore, to make an accurate record of the basis on which advice is given. It is also a sensible precaution to write to the client setting out the foundation on which litigation is to be commenced.

A classic area involving fact witnesses in criminal cases is identification. That identification witnesses are fallible is easily demonstrable. It is a well known trick during the first year of Law School to stage an incident in which a stranger enters a lecture theatre and argues publicly with the lecturer. The stranger leaves and the class is asked to make notes on the stranger's appearance. They disagree, sometimes fundamentally, and the point is made; identification by witnesses is frequently unreliable.

In 1976 Peter Hain, well known at the time for a high profile campaign against sporting and financial links with South Africa, was charged with robbery from a bank. He had gone shopping for a typewriter ribbon and was identified by three boys as a robber who, moments before, they had chased with a bank official. Hain's vehicle number was given to the police by the boys and he was arrested. He was identified in a parade by the teller from whom the money was snatched. The bank official who chased him failed to identify him. Hain's book, 'Mistaken Identity', is a good 'insider's view' of the system at work. Since that time guidelines have been laid down for the acceptance of uncorroborated and challenged identification evidence (see *Turnbull* [1977] QB 224 and Codes of Practice made under the Police and Criminal Evidence Act (1984) covering the conduct of identification parades).

The first question for the advocate in an identification case is, therefore, 'is this witness likely to tell the truth as they see it? If they have no reason to lie and their evidence is adverse the advocate must consider the possibility of challenging the witness' memory of the incident. A plan for cross-examination of identification witnesses might include the following matters:

- the time elapsed since the incident and the implications for memory

- any physical disability; poor eyesight, for example

- the duration of the incident

- the general conditions under which the events were observed; light, distance etc

- the specific conditions for that witness; the view that the witness had on the event, for example

- the amount of activity in the area in general (was this an offence where the witness' attention would be drawn to the defendant?)

- any personal threat to the witness which may have interfered with perception

- dramatic events which made the witness' attention to minor details unlikely

- the possibility of confusion with previous or subsequent events

- the circumstances under which identification took place

- the possibility of pressure on the witness

- the suggestibility of the witness (for example an indication to an identification witness that 'Mr X is the one')

Exercise One

If you were acting as the defence advocate in Hain's case, what would be your general strategy and which areas might be profitably pursued in cross-examining:

- the boys who gave chase and
- the bank teller?

Devise two key questions for each line of enquiry. What difference would it make if the three boys had been overheard discussing 'the chase' outside the courtroom, 'as if they were trying to agree about what they had seen'?

(You will find a small section from both these cross-examinations in the final Chapter.)

3.3.2   Opinion evidence

Expert evidence is used in a large number of cases and its possible relevance to any case should always be considered. The function of experts is, 'inter alia, to explain words or terms of science or art appearing on the documents which have to be construed by the court, to give expert assistance to the court (eg as to the laws of science or the working of a technical process or system) or to inform the court as to the state of public knowledge with regard to the matters before it' (Rules of the Supreme Court Order 38 Rule 4/2).

Even if you are acting for a client whose washing machine has broken down there may be issues which can only be determined by an expert. Was the machine abused? Was it faulty? How long could it be expected to last without repair? It many cases the opinions of experts for either side will diverge in one or more crucial respects. All other evidence being equal one or other expert opinion may decide the case. While it is not always the case, the more elevated the expert the more credibility she will have, at least at the start of the case.

In preparing your own case you will often need to work closely with your expert. In instructing an expert you should provide copies of all original documents and details of where physical evidence can be inspected. Remember that the expert is coming fresh to the case and will appreciate a letter from you which explains the issues. The expert's opinion will be based on the evidence you provide. If your expert has to admit in cross-examination that they did not see an important document, or a particular piece of equipment, the evidence they give will be undermined.

Depending on the type of case it may be that you will need to cross-examine an expert on the other side. You need to understand enough about the expert's specialism to make cross examination possible. Your expert is the key to unlocking this knowledge. By discussing the other expert's report in conference your expert can point out unjustified assumptions, technical errors and illogical deductions. It may be necessary for you to read around the subject; your expert will be able to suggest introductory texts which will save you time and effort. Ask your own expert whether they are aware of anything written by the other side's expert on the topic in issue. You may find an occasion when they have expressed views which contradict the views they have expressed in your case. Do not be embarrassed to put yourself in your expert's hands; you are a lawyer, not a washing machine repairer. If you begin to specialise in a particular area you should consider supplementing your law library with books in the relevant discipline. You will soon save time and effort by understanding and anticipating the expert's needs.

Anticipate that each side will adopt a different focus in presenting their expert evidence. In a personal injury claim, for example, the plaintiff's advocate will use medical evidence to emphasise:

- the nature and effect of the injuries
- any causal connection with the accident
- the duration of the injuries
- any expenses incurred and likely to be incurred

- any impairment of earning capacity

In contrast, the defendant's focus in presenting the medical evidence will be:

- the lack of causal link between accident and symptoms
- invalid assumptions made by the plaintiff's expert
- exaggeration of symptoms
- the lack of support for the plaintiff's claims of incapacity
- the capacity of the plaintiff to continue his previous employment or to find another (equally) well paid job

Anticipating the different emphasis of each expert will suggest the matters to investigate and discuss with your expert.

3.4   Developing a hypothesis

In preparing a case you need to be thorough and make efficient use of your time. If you are familiar with the facts because you have been involved with the case from the start the task is easier. However, it is still necessary to thoroughly review the file, even when you are familiar with the issues.

Sometimes you may receive a bundle of papers just prior to a court appearance.

There are many ways of reviewing materials. I recommend the following:

- skim read the documents for familiarisation. Make a mind map or some other form of outline of the main issues
- number the pages of your bundle
- go through the papers again and make a chronological list of important events noting in each case the number of the document containing the relevant material

Remember that when a case goes to court there may be different bundles of documents. There will be those which the parties have agreed, and need not be proved by witnesses, and separate bundles of plaintiff's and defendant's documents which have not been agreed by the other side. If you do not have responsibility for preparing any of these bundles you should check the numbering of each bundle with the other side. This will enable the judge, witnesses and advocates to conveniently find the documents in each bundle as you refer to them

• Create a working hypothesis

Your working hypothesis is based on the available facts. It should take account of those facts which are in dispute. The framework is provided by the facts which are agreed by the parties or by their experts and the facts which are corroborated by agreed documents or physical evidence. A lawyer is generally concerned with material facts, that is, those facts which must be proved to establish a cause of action or a conviction. However, facts which may not appear to be material may throw light on other evidence. It is sensible not to reject facts as irrelevant too early in your preparation. Nor is it sensible to become wed to any one hypothesis at an early stage. As you collect evidence you may find yourself prematurely rejecting evidence which conflicts with your hypothesis. Try to remain open minded for as long as possible. If more than one hypothesis is consistent with the facts you have, suspend judgement until you know more. It may be quite late in a civil case that you are able to see the whole picture. In most cases you will be able to compare the other side's expert reports and witness statements with your own.

You will be able to access a range of information on factual disputes which was not available to previous generations of lawyers. Use it well. In planning for advocacy do not be blinded to the risks of going to court and to the arguments for a negotiated settlement. Remember to warn the client of the risks, make sure that the client understands your advice and obtain clear instructions. The obligation to disclose fact evidence should lead to an even larger number of settlements and you need to be constantly aware of this possibility.

In considering your hypothesis ask yourself these questions:

- is this hypothesis consistent with the facts as known to me?
- is this hypothesis likely to be credible to a disinterested observer?
- is there any evidence inconsistent with this account?
- can the hypothesis be amended or changed to accommodate contradictory evidence or must the evidence be challenged?
- what else do I need to know to prove or disprove this hypothesis?
- if this hypothesis is correct, what is the likely legal outcome?

You may find it useful to represent the case in a logical diagrammatic form at this stage. The following diagram is adapted from student materials used by the Law Society of Upper Canada.

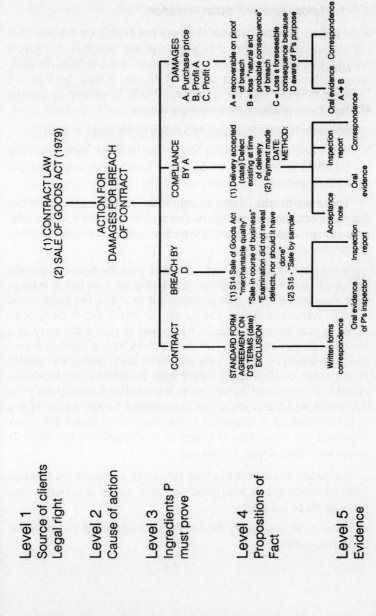

Level 1
Source of clients
Legal right

(1) CONTRACT LAW
(2) SALE OF GOODS ACT (1979)

Level 2
Cause of action

ACTION FOR
DAMAGES FOR BREACH
OF CONTRACT

Level 3
Ingredients P
must prove

CONTRACT   BREACH BY   COMPLIANCE   DAMAGES
                            D   BY A   A. Purchase price
                                                                    B. Profit A
                                                                    C. Profit C

A = recoverable on proof
    of breach
B = loss "natural and
    probable consequence"
    of breach
C = Loss a foreseeable
    consequence because
    D aware of P's purpose

Level 4
Propositions of
Fact

STANDARD FORM
AGREEMENT ON
D'S TERMS (date)
EXCLUSION

(1) S14 Sale of Goods Act
"merchantable quality"
"Sale in course of business"
"Examination did not reveal
defects, nor should it have
'done'"
(2) S15 - "Sale by sample"

(1) Delivery accepted
(date) Defect
existing at time
of delivery
(2) Payment made
DATE:
METHOD:

Level 5
Evidence

Written forms
correspondence

Oral evidence
of P's inspector

Inspection
report

Acceptance
note

Oral
evidence

Inspection
report   Correspondence

Oral evidence   Correspondence
A → B

3.4.1   Legal and technical disputes

If it appears that the material facts are not in dispute the advocate should consider whether it is a point of law which is in issue. It may be that the defence does not consider that the facts pleaded, even if proven, reveal a cause of action. It may be that the defence believes that the courts are ready to extend or change the law. Having anticipated the legal issues:

* consider how well precedent applies to the case in hand
* anticipate the other side's argument (and the best means of rebutting it) and consider how your client's own argument can best be put

Legal points can often be argued in the alternative (whether cause of action or remedy). However, it is important to consider whether an argument in the alternative can be advanced without undermining credibility.

It is possible that the other side has no substantive argument on either fact or law. They may be relying on a technical error in your preparation. It is always important to check the papers and rules of procedure before the hearing to see if errors have been made. It may be that the court has power to rectify the error at a hearing. On the other hand an amendment may constitute a new cause of action or involve new parties; in such cases the powers of the court to allow amendment may be affected by limitation. Where amendment raises new issues the hearing may be adjourned and the costs of the amendment thrown away. In any of these cases it is important to be alert to the possibilities, not least that the other side is aware of a procedural error which is becoming more serious by the day.

If you identify a possible technical error, research the relevant rules of procedure to see whether the situation is covered. Ask yourself these questions:

* if the court can rectify the error what matters will be taken into consideration?

- are there any cases reported in which the facts were similar and, if so, what were the determining factors in those cases?

- should the court be asked to rectify the error or do I need to vacate or adjourn the hearing and take remedial steps?

3.4.2 Ulterior motives

Some reasons for cases going to court may have little to do with the merits of the case as such. The defamed or the 'wronged spouse' may want their day in court. Institutional defendants, such as insurance companies, may rely on some claimants not pursuing a case to trial. Some solicitors pride themselves on running cases to the door of the court in the hope of securing a better negotiated settlement. Debtors may want to buy time for their business's cash flow to improve. You may be able to guess what lies behind a desire to proceed with a poor case and deal with it in advance. I once had a case where the insurers revealed that the plaintiff for whom I was acting had fraudulently claimed car hire expenses. They thought that doubts created about the plaintiff's credibility would undermine claims about his continuing medical problems. My litigation partner wisely wrote an open letter withdrawing the expenses claim. The potential damage was limited and the plaintiff still managed to recover more than the sum paid into court by the defence.

The client may be able to help you to identify ulterior motives. If you suspect the other side of pursuing litigation for the wrong reasons, this information might be put to use in several ways. The debtor who is delaying payment may concede the action if ordered to pay the disputed sum into court. This may condition your approach in an application for summary judgment where there appears to be an arguable defence. The plaintiff who wants his day in court may be receptive to arguments, assurances and solutions which are better generated through negotiation. The institutional defendant may be more prepared to compromise if convinced of the plaintiff's determination to proceed with the action. Also, if any witness stands to gain from proceedings it is important to bring this out in direct evidence.

Finally, it may be appropriate to use insight into a party's motive in the conduct of a hearing. Courts and tribunals are often affected by 'the merits' of a case, that is, the social or moral weight of the argument as opposed to the weight of legal argument.

> '... the facts set up an emotional or cardiac reaction in the judicial mind and heart. The judge's reaction is either, the plaintiff ought to win, let me see if the law permits such a result, or, the defendant ought to win if the law will allow it. The law being what it is, living and fluid, you generally find what you are looking for'.

> Rifkind (1984)

3.5   A theory of the case

Having looked at your working hypothesis from every angle and discovered as much as you can about the other side's case you are ready to formulate your theory of the case.

> 'The theory of the case is the basic, underlying idea that explains not only the legal theory and factual background, but also fits as much of the evidence as possible into a coherent and credible whole'.

> McElhaney (1979)

Let us briefly return to the Hain case to illustrate this idea. The defence theory of the case is as follows:-

Peter Hain was incorrectly identified by four witnesses as having committed a robbery. There is no other evidence against him and there are witnesses who had a better view of the robber and who say that Hain was not the man. Three of the adverse witnesses are boys who chased the robber. Their identification is suspect because the robber was running away and they did not have a clear opportunity to see him for any length of time. They incorrectly identified Hain in the bookshop because he bears a passing resemblance to the robber. Their description of the robber is based on their subsequent sighting of Hain. They support each other in their error; their recollection may have been shaped by questioning and they may have been suggestible. The bank teller was under personal threat at the time of the robbery and this interfered with her perception. She picked out Hain in an identification parade because she had seen Hain on the television that and knew that he had been arrested in connection with the offence.

To some extent the advocate must predict what will be proved in evidence. Because of the possibility of different findings of fact you may need to develop more than one theory of the case. Obviously credibility is damaged if these competing theories of the case are not consistent with each other. The problem for the advocate in presenting more than one theory of the case is to remain convincing while presenting a message to which she is not committed.

Any theory of the case must be able to withstand rigorous testing. Preparation should include an analysis of the other side's strengths. You can even try to anticipate or discover their theory of the case. This will help to reduce the risk of surprise at trial and alert you to possible weak spots in the case you have to answer.

When you have developed your working hypothesis into a theory of the case you will need to think about:

- reinforcing your own weak points

- making best use of your strengths

- deciding whether you need to attack the other side's strengths and, if you must, the best way to do it

- how to make the best use of the other sides weaknesses

As you expand your theory of the case you will want to test it. In doing so you will wish to uncover what Binder & Bergman (1984) call 'additional events' which help to fill out a chronology. These provide context and are a crucial stage in the development of both theory and narrative.

'An 'event' inquiry typically concerns an occurrence at a discrete moment in time: a topic inquiry typically calls attention to certain

subject matter and searches for moments in time when that subject matter occurred. In a sense, a topical enquiry divorces an event from the moment of its occurrence. For instance, topical questions might be 'Did you ever talk to the manager about sparks coming from the sink?' or 'Did your company suffer any losses as a result of your suppliers' failure to send the explosives?'. If a witness answers either question affirmatively, one may expand the story by uncovering the specific event or events giving rise to the response. For example, if the witness responds that losses did occur, one may then ask the witness to identify specific incidents of loss.'

                                                                Binder and Bergman (1984)

Since particular topics or events will not appear significant when you start your investigation further attendances on witnesses may be necessary to elaborate proofs of evidence in this way. Obviously your strategy will generally be to play to your strengths and weaken the other side's strengths; you can anticipate, for example, that you are unlikely to cross-examine an excellent witness for the other side unless you have the material to either destroy or at least neutralise their evidence.

3.6   Organising materials

Materials need to be organised in the way in which you will present your case to the court. Having identified the best order, you should follow that sequence as far as possible in your opening speech, your presentation of witnesses and, again, in your closing speech. In this way you will gain the benefit of reinforcement.

Glickman identifies four different possibilities for presenting facts:

- Chronological order ie the order in which events occurred

- Topical order ie the order dictated by some outside requirement eg establishing duty, breach and damage

- Logical order ie is there a problem? what is the nature of the problem? what is the cause of the problem?

- An order building to an 'inevitable conclusion' - so that, if the facts are accepted, there is only one possible outcome

Glickman (1982)

There are several advantages to this last format because it incorporates both sides of the story, both good and bad points, works from common ground and gradually fits in the pieces of the story. The audience is filling the pieces in, as you proceed, wanting to see you complete the puzzle.

3.7   Keeping materials

It is dangerous to have badly organised materials. You may not be able to find what you want when you need it. You will go down in the estimation of the court and the client as you hunt through your materials for the document you need. If you continually lose your thread you will feel less and less confident and, as a result, you will be less able to do a competent job.

A good idea, originating in the United States, is to keep a 'trial notebook'. The most convenient form is a ring binder containing:

- a table of contents (but marked by colour sections rather than numerically; you need to be able to take things out without upsetting your order)

- the case analysis including:
  - your theory of the case

  - an analysis of the other side's case and probable theory of the case

  - a proof checklist containing three columns

Elements to be proved	Supporting evidence	Source of evidence

    Column three should include a page number of any agreed bundle of documents

- Documents and Exhibits
- Research notes - argument on particularly difficult points
- Closing speech

McElhaney (1980)

3.8   Finally - narrative or story-telling

Binder & Bergman suggest that the decisive factor in most cases is the plausibility of the story outline presented by each side, not the detailed evidence given by witnesses.

> 'for a story to appear credible not only must the crucial events be related to one another in a coherent manner, but also the telling of those events must be accompanied by some contextual detail, which is itself irrelevant to the base story-line, but nevertheless places it in a context recognisable to the audience. At the same time they stress that not too much detail should be provided; the base story line must not be submerged ...'

Jackson (1988)

The final stage of preparation is to turn the theory of the case into a story; to build it up again from the bare legal bones to a fully dressed narrative. If you have approached the initial client interview with the need to 'dress' your case you will have rich resources of imagery to plunder. If not, it is never too late to go over your theory of the case with the client clarifying the detail and refreshing the memory. This is not just window dressing; it is important for all the material details of the location, the actors and the events to be visualised by all participants in the proceedings. The advocate's first objective must be for her theory of the case to be fully understood by the judge or jury.

When examining your own witnesses thought must be given to the potential impact of the 'narrative mode' which is made possible by open rather than closed questions. When cross-examining, a strong mental picture of the facts is essential. It enables you to respond quickly to witnesses' answers and not be tied to set questions. The area of cross examination should be identified in advance issue by issue. If you find it helpful an opening question in relation to each issue can be written out. Better still, the key question to which you are building can be included under each heading.

Exercise Two

In the next three Chapters I shall be using extracts from the trial of Alfred Arthur Rouse. The basic facts are as follows:

Rouse was accused of murdering an unknown man at around 2 am on November 6th 1930 outside the little village of Hardingstone near Northampton. Rouse was a commercial traveller who claimed that he was travelling from London to the Midlands in order to draw some money from his employers' offices there. His story was that before leaving London, he was hailed by a respectable looking man who asked for a lift to the Midlands. Rouse agreed to give him a lift. During the journey a police constable drew Rouse's attention to a defective light on his car. Just outside a Hardingstone, a village near Northampton 'the engine began to spit. Rouse said 'I thought I was running out of petrol'. Rouse got out of the car in order to 'relieve himself' and, showing his companion a petrol can, suggested that he top up the tank. The man asked for a cigarette. Rouse, pointing out that the man had smoked his last one, offered him a cigar. The man told Rouse that he did not need a light. Rouse went some distance down the road and was about to return to the car when there was a terrible explosion.

He panicked, running up Hardingstone Lane towards the village. Two young men, Bailey and Brown, were walking home from a dance. As they turned into Hardingstone Lane a car ran along the main road linking Northampton and London. Almost simultaneously they saw a man and the blaze in the distance. The man passed them going towards the village of Hardingstone and the main road. Bailey asked Brown what he thought the blaze was and, as if in answer, the stranger said 'it looks as if someone is having a bonfire up there'. They observed the stranger stop at the end of the lane seeming confused about which direction to take.

Rouse hitched a lift back to London not mentioning the events in Hardingstone to anyone. He visited his wife briefly and then caught a coach to Wales to visit a young woman whom he had made pregnant and promised to marry. While he was there he saw a newspaper with the account of the 'blazing car'. After two days he returned to London and was arrested on his arrival. He told police:

'I had just got my trousers up quickly and ran towards the car which was in flames. I saw the man was inside and I tried to open the door, but could not as the car was a mass of flames ... I felt I was responsible for what happened. I lost my head and did not know what to do and really don't know what I have done since.'

The corpse of the unknown man was found in the front seat of the car. His identity was not discovered. Rouse claimed not to have asked his name. Photographs of the corpse were taken only after some delay and the body's exact position immediately after the fire was surmised from sometimes conflicting accounts of police officers. It was accepted however, that the head was face down in the driver's seat with the trunk across the passenger seat. It was probable that one leg had hung outside the passenger door. The car was faced in the direction of the village. The fire had been particularly severe and had apparently been sustained by a steady flow of petrol. Examination of the burnt out wreck revealed that the petrol can was in the rear seat of the car, the carburettor lid was not in place (which would cause the carburettor to fill with petrol and overflow) and the nut on the petrol union joint was loose.

- Make a mind map of the issues as they appear to you from this very brief summary.

- What do you think should be the prosecution theory of the case? What are the elements of that case and the evidence which might support them?

3.9 Summary

In preparing for advocacy you must identify:

- what facts are in dispute
- what law is relevant
- what evidence supports your client's version of events
- what evidence is missing and how it can be obtained
- what you need to establish at the hearing
- what is your working hypothesis for the case (later to become your 'theory of the case')
- whether there any procedural errors or drafting errors in the documents which should be drawn to the attention of the court, the impact of any error and the court's power to remedy the defect
- your theory (or theories) of the case and the best way of presenting it (or them)
- whether the documentation is complete and conveniently organised for the purpose

3.10   End of chapter references and additional reading

Bastress R M and Harbaugh J D (1990)	*Interviewing, Counselling & Negotiating* *Skills for Effective Presentation* Parts 1-3 Little, Brown & Co
Bettle J (1992)	*Personal Injury Claims in the County Court* Fourmat Publishing
Binder D and Bergman P (1984)	*Fact Investigation* West Publishing
Bowers J (1987-8)	*Presenting a case in the Industrial* *Tribunal: A Practical Approach* Litigation Vol 7
Frank J (1949)	*Courts on Trial: Myth and Reality in* *American Justice* Ch 3 Princeton University Press
Glickman J (1982)	*Persuasion in Litigation* Litigation Vol 8 No 3
Jackson B S (1988)	*Law, Narrative and Fact Coherence* Deborah Charles
McElhaney J W (1979)	*The Theory of the Case* Litigation Vol 6 No 1
McElhaney J W (1980)	*The Trial Note Book* Litigation Vol 1 No 1
Morrison J and Leith P (1992)	*The Barrister's World and the Nature of Law* Ch 5 Open University Press

Napley D (1991)	*The Technique of Persuasion* Ch 1 Sweet & Maxwell
J and Hill R	*Civil Litigation* Longman
Rifkind S H (1984)	*How to Try a Non-Jury* Litigation Vol 10 No 3
Stone M (1988)	*Cross-Examination in Criminal Trials* Ch 2 Butterworths
Zuckermann A A S (1989)	*The Principles of Criminal Evidence* Chs 2 - 3 Clarendon Press

CHAPTER

4 Opening

'... a cause requires that the expectations of the audience should be met with all possible expedition; and if nothing to satisfy them be offered at the commencement, much more labour is necessary in the sequel.'

Cicero 'De Oratore'

4.1 Introductions

An opening speech will introduce the issues in the order determined by the advocate. In general an opening should introduce the facts in the order in which they will emerge in the evidence. Advocates generally have discretion in the selection and order of presentation of witnesses (Rules of the Supreme Court Order 38 Rule 1(3)). The obvious order may be chronological. The aim is that the judge or jury should be given the best opportunity to understand your case; the repetition of your chosen sequence, in opening and through the order in which witnesses are called, will help them to do this. In addition, the sequence should be logical. Departing from the logical sequence should only occur where this is necessary, for example, starting or ending with your strongest witness.

Lawyers need to make different kinds of speeches for different purposes and for different audiences. A speech introducing a case to a jury will be of a different character than a speech introducing a case to a master or judge. If the speech is by way of introduction to an application the lawyer will be guided by the Master or Judge who is hearing the application.

In all cases you should introduce yourself and the other advocate, if any. At many courts you will hand a slip with your name on to the usher. If you do you this you need not give your name in your introduction. It is still common for advocates to commence by saying:

'If it please you (Your Honour), I appear for the plaintiff in this case. Mr Bumptious appears for the defence'.

There are several ways you can then proceed. On applications or summonses your speech could then be broken by a polite enquiry as to how the judge would like you to proceed, such as, 'would Your Honour like me to read the plaintiff's affidavit?'. However, reading out an affidavit can be a tedious process and, if the affidavit has been filed in advance, it has probably been read. A more satisfactory approach is to outline in your own words the purpose of the application and the issues, propose a course of action and then pause for guidance from the judge.

In other cases, opening speeches in a trial, for example, the speech will be longer and uninterrupted. In it, the lawyer will be expected to set out her case to the court. In either case brevity and conciseness is usually appreciated. Because of the primacy effect any opening should have the maximum impact. The advocate must be at her best; fluent, persuasive and concise. The opening speech should be practised and refined so that it can be delivered with verve and purpose.

> 'To be confused in memory, or to lose our fluency of speech, has nowhere a worse effect than at the commencement. The pilot is surely one of the worst who runs his vessel aground as it is leaving the harbour'
>
> Quintillian 'Institutes of Oratory'

There is a lot to be said for directing the court towards the desired conclusion. A sense of purpose, a clear indication of aims, can be highly persuasive:

> 'If I am doing court work I want to be thoroughly prepared and to have thought about my goal and how I will convince the court to give me what I want. I try to be concise and relevant. I start by saying what I want and why; people know up front what I am after

... Nowadays I see more young barristers around who are use this format so I assume they are being taught that way. The problem is that they are slow and long-winded; they add far too much detail. That will be lost with experience'.

A Solicitor advocate quoted in Boon (1992)

The goal of the opening speech, whatever the context, will be to create a positive and persuasive first impression. Inevitably, however, different considerations apply to making openings in different courts and contexts.

4.2   Criminal courts

In criminal cases the prosecution offers its evidence first. Only if this shows a case to answer will the defence need to offer its own evidence. Not every court offers the same opportunity to make a speech introducing the case. In magistrates courts both prosecution and defence are allowed only one speech. The prosecution introduces the case, usually with a brief speech, and the defence usually makes a closing speech. What follows will concentrate on openings in the crown court before a jury (for Magistrates Courts see Stone's Justices' Manual 1992).

In the Crown Court the prosecution will make an opening speech. The defence is only entitled to make an opening speech if calling witnesses to fact other than the accused. The defence opening speech is made after the prosecution has called all its evidence. It is almost a convention that a defence opening in the Crown Court is brief; often it is foregone altogether. In the US the 'opening statement' is rarely waived because of belief in the critical importance of the 'primacy effect' on a jury, that is, that the first thing you say makes the deepest impression. According to Lindquist,

'opening speeches determine the outcome of trials more than 50% of the time. Indeed respectable studies indicate it may be

85% of the time. While other parts of the trial confirm it, opening statements give the jury a basic feeling for who is right and why, who has the better facts, what is the logical result'.

Lindquist (1982)

Norman Birkett QC, whose opening speech in the Rouse trial will be considered shortly, was also conscious of the importance of an opening speech and of the primacy effect:

'The jury fresh to the court, fresh to the case, hear a presentation, and they are never, never likely to forget. Shaken they may be by cross-examination, by subsequent witnesses but that first, clear, incisive impression made upon the jury is beyond all price.

Birkett (1948)

4.3   Style

Making a speech to a jury presents special problems for a lawyer. Obviously the use of legal jargon may be alienating; sometimes legal concepts may need to be explained because they are central to the case. However, legal 'terms of art' should be avoided. Aim for a tone which is almost conversational.

'Eloquence ... in the sense of careful and precise language is crucial. The word choice must be clear, direct and appropriate, varied, interesting, often very conversational and always direct and communicative

Lindquist (1982)

Avoid being seen to 'talk down' to the jury, do not feel that you must 'impress':

'A mode of delivery in which all art is concealed, and which, as the Greeks say, is 'unostentatious' steals most successfully in the mind of the hearer'

Quintillian 'Institutes of Oratory'

Mannerisms should be avoided; attention should be focused on what you are saying not the way you stroke your nose or pat your hair.

It is always necessary to convey conviction and this is particularly so with juries. The jurors have to care about this trial; they won't if the advocate cannot. Do not write a prepared speech: working from an outline or map will enable you to face the jurors and seek eye to eye contact with as many as possible. Do not concentrate on one to the exclusion of others although, if you are able to identify potential leaders, more eye contact with those individuals may be justified. Demand the juries respect; do not be servile to your opponent or the court and state the problems in your case honestly.

Julien (1985)

4.4   Structuring prosecution openings

4.4.1   Introductions

Introduce yourself, the other advocate/s and the case. Try to be comfortable with the jury, aim to be helpful to them, for example by explaining their role in the proceedings. Predicting what will happen will give them confidence in you when it does; for example, 'There will be technical evidence and it may appear dull, but it is crucial to the case.'

4.4.2   Summarise the facts

One aim of the opening speech is to enable the audience to visualise the events and to place the central issues of fact within these events. It is important not to obscure the main issues with inconsequential detail. During the first few minutes of the opening a jury is attentive, receptive and curious about the case. If your theory of the case is powerfully explained at this point it will stick in the collective memory. However, the advocate also needs to secure and retain interest by humanising the story. Lawyers in the United States often use rhetorical questions to stimulate interest in their client:

> *'Ladies and gentlemen of the jury, you must be asking yourself, who is my client and what does he want? I represent Roger Fry. He is a young man. He is what is called a blue collar worker. He works with his hands. He liked working long hours as a steamfitter. What does he want from this lawsuit? He wants to justify your decision to give money damages ...'*

> Stein (1977)

Narrative can also be used in court to great effect. In the Chapter on Planning, one aspect of the power of narrative was explained. Norman Birkett QC is recognised as one of the leading advocates of his era. Consider the narrative skill, the atmosphere of suspicion and menace, evoked in his opening speech in the Rouse trial. Some key words are italicised in the excerpt below. What is the purpose of these words in the context of this extract?

> '... Two young men walking home from a dance met the accused just after they had turned into Hardingstone Lane ... It was an *early morning*, *bright* and *moonlit* and as they reached that junction on the farther side of the lane from which they stood, they saw a rather *remarkable* sight. They saw *the prisoner* come out from the direction of a ditch on the side of the road, *hatless and carrying an attache case*. There, from that *strange place*, at that *strange time*, on that *lonely road*, the accused emerged ...'

4.4.3   State the issues of fact

These are the material facts on which the case turns. It is increasingly recognised that logical argument alone does not convince juries. A study of 600 jury trials in the US support the idea that juries rarely see a case in the same way a lawyer would. Lawyers are trained to think cognitively, that is, logically and abstractly, and to conceptualise and evaluate argument from a number of different perspectives. People without this training or background may think affectively, that is from feelings and set points of view. Affective thinkers tend to reject information inconsistent with their opinions. They certainly do not seek it out.

Cognitive thinkers will not reject or be prejudiced against an affective argument while affective thinkers need an argument which appeals to their emotions. They will not appreciate and may not forgive a cognitive argument. This analysis supports the use of 'psychological anchors' in jury trials. 'Psychological anchors' are issues of fact so significant that the members of the jury will always remember them. Affective thinkers on the jury will use them to organise subsequent details and to make sense of the conflicting evidence they hear. Cognitive thinkers may also use psychological anchors where the issues and evidence are complex.

A case which illustrated the effective use of a psychological anchor concerned an action for damages over a drowning at a swimming pool. When the deceased was pulled from the pool it was noted by several witnesses that her arm was blue from wrist to shoulder. None of the doctors called to give evidence could explain it. The plaintiff's case focused on the adequacy of safety measures. The defence, however, pre-tried the case with a shadow jury and found that they were troubled by this aspect of the case. It was made a major issue in the opening address by the defendant's lawyer. The defendants won. The blue arm had no apparent legal significance but the jury believed that the blue arm indicated some unexplained medical trauma. They concluded that the woman had lost consciousness and drowned.

Vinson (1985)

Birkett's opening speech in the Rouse trial demonstrates an intuitive understanding of the psychological anchor. Before you reach the end of the passage you should have a very clear idea of the single fact which Birkett wanted the jury to remember above all else.

'... After they had passed one of them said 'What is the blaze up there?' pointing to a glare up the lane, and then, having gone 15 or 20 yards beyond the men, the accused said these very remarkable words: 'It looks as if someone is having a bonfire up there'. Members of the jury, you will hear what was found up that lane. You will hear the accused's part in it, and you will bear in mind at every stage of this case the fact that, right at the outset, when the accused met those two young men, he passed without a word. No appeal for help! No call for assistance! Nothing. And then 'It looks as though someone is having a bonfire up there'. You will hear that what he called a bonfire was the burning of his own car; and that there was the body of that unknown man in that car being steadily burned beyond all recognition. The significance of the remark 'It looks as though someone is having a bonfire up there' cannot be over-emphasised in view of the fact that 400 yards away there was that terrible fire. The car had shortly before been drawn up by the side of the road by the prisoner himself; he had shut off the engine and put on the brake ... and yet, at that moment, his observation to these two young men was 'It looks as if someone has had a bonfire' ...'

The use of the phrase 'It looks as if someone has had a bonfire up there' is a clear illustration of repetition for effect. There is no inspiration failure here! The whole passage is carefully constructed around a systematic return to that single sentence. Why? The prosecution's theory of the case is that Rouse's conduct after the conflagration was inconsistent with his innocence. His words are not those of a man seized by panic.

Notice also the direct language and constant grouping of words and phrases in 'threes'.

4.4.4   Outline admissible evidence

Prosecutors benefit from the use of direct language. Instead of saying, 'the witness will say he saw ...' or, 'I was not there but the witnesses will tell you ...', say, 'Mr Green saw ... ' If there is an objection that you are representing evidence as fact preface what you say with 'we will prove that ...' Be careful what you say will be proved; if your evidence fails to fulfil expectations the competent defence will expose that failure. You are making a commitment to the jury and you must fully expect to meet that commitment. Promise only what you can deliver.

In the next extract from Birkett's opening speech he introduces the expert evidence he will call. There are two devices in this short passage with which Birkett aims to stimulate interest in this crucial evidence:

'This fire was undoubtedly one of intensity and fierceness. How did it start? Where did it start? Was there anything in the remains of the car which will help you to answer that question? There was. I will call before you a witness, Colonel Buckle, who has very wide experience of fires in motor cars and fires generally. To summarise his conclusions he will say ...'

(If in doubt look back at 1.8)

• Presenting strengths

English lawyers are often advised to 'keep their powder dry'; to save strong evidence so as to surprise the other side. Lawyers in the United States are often advised not to do this. Such is the belief in the effect of the opening speech on a jury that lawyers are usually advised to present the strongest case possible. You can never be sure that the jury will appreciate the subtleties of the evidence.

• Confronting weaknesses

If you anticipate that the defence will make much of a weakness in your case it is often best to forewarn the jury of the difficulty and present it in the best light possible. In the Rouse case, Birkett confronted the problem that the evidence against Rouse was largely circumstantial. People are convicted on circumstantial evidence all the time. However, where evidence is circumstantial a case is considerably bolstered by proof of motive. Making this point is the other advocate's job. Birkett does not dwell on the difficulty; he does not concede this weakness in his own case or compromise the impact of what he says. In fact, at one point he asserts that circumstantial evidence may be better (almost) than direct evidence. I think the 'almost' was a mistake!

> 'The grave offence of wilful murder, by the very nature of the case, is seldom committed where human eyes might behold, relate and report ... what is called direct evidence is sometimes difficult and sometimes impossible to obtain. The evidence which is brought in this case is what is known as circumstantial evidence. But circumstantial evidence might be of such texture, such strength, such cogency, as to be superior almost to direct evidence. From the evidence it is proposed to call before you, from the logic of the circumstances and from the facts here you will be led *to one conclusion, and to one conclusion only*, and that is that the unknown man in that car, on that road, on that day, was murdered by the accused ...'

Note the simple use of parallel phrases (italicised) for emphasis and the repeated use of words or phrases in groups of three. Compare Birkett's introduction to circumstantial evidence with the analogy an American lawyer, Craig Spangenburg, habitually uses to explain the concept to juries:

> 'This reminds me of my father reading Robinson Crusoe to me when I was a little boy. Remember, when Robinson Crusoe was on the island for such a long time alone? One morning he went down to the beach and there was a footprint on the sand. He was so overcome with emotion, he fainted. And why did he faint? Did he see a man? He woke to find Friday standing beside him, who was to be his friend on the island, but he did not see Friday. Did he see a foot? No. He saw a footprint. That is, he saw marks in the sand, the kind of marks that are made by a human foot. He saw circumstantial evidence. But it was true, it was valid, it was compelling, as it would be to all of you. We live with it in our lives. So let's look at the facts of this case - for those tracks which prove the truth ...'

What are the possible objectives of the advocate in explaining 'circumstantial evidence' to the jury? Bearing in mind possible objectives, which of these two explanations of circumstantial evidence do you think would be more appropriate? You may wish to compare these extracts with the example from <u>Exall</u> in Chapter Two at para 2.8 and with a text book definition (see, for example, May on Criminal Evidence (1990)). The use of analogy is obviously a technique to arouse interest and to make a new concept accessible. How many other examples of 'presentation technique' can you see in this second extract?

Birkett produced little or no evidence as to motive in the Rouse trial. Yet he used the power of suggestion in his opening, asking the jury to draw an inference from the evidence which would be presented. Notice how in this part of his opening speech Birkett uses less direct language.

'... You might think that there never could be an adequate motive for murder ... You might think that the facts and the circumstances in this case pointed to the conclusion - that for some reason the accused desired the charred remains of that unknown man to be taken for his, and that when he had emerged out of the hedge at that hour in the morning and had been seen by two young men, the plan or design might have miscarried ...'

Notice the use of the qualifying 'You might think' before the suggested motive. This is very tentative phraseology. Notice also how, shortly before, Birkett had used 'You might think' to preface a proposition with which the jury must, inevitably, agree. Do you think that was deliberate? If so, to what end?

One final point on confronting weaknesses. If you deal with problems by forewarning the jury it is sensible to hide these points in the middle of the speech. As we have seen, less attention will be paid to what is said in the middle than at the beginning or end.

4.4.5   Outline the legal issues

The judge will direct the jury on the law at the conclusion of the case and it is as well to remind the jury of that. However, unless the jury is helped by being given some simple foundation in law, particular points may bother them throughout the trial. See how Birkett guides the jury on the significance of motive. What do you think he means in the italicised section? If his meaning is obscure, was this deliberate?

> 'One of the questions that might arise in your minds is that of motive. His lordship will guide you on the law in that case, and you will accept the law from him. But I think that the learned judge will tell you that *motive is immaterial from one point of view* and that it is no part of the duty of the prosecution to supply to the jury a satisfying, adequate or, indeed, any motive'

4.5   Structuring Defence openings

At the conclusion of prosecution evidence the defence can make an opening speech if witnesses as to fact are to be called. The defence advocate should indicate that this is the case by saying 'Your Honour, I shall be calling other evidence'. An argument for not using this opportunity is that you may wish to keep evidence as a surprise in order to increase its impact. However, a persuasive argument against this is that members of a jury may well miss the significance of evidence unless the defence theory of the case is first firmly fixed in their minds. There is one rule of criminal evidence which provides a constraint in terms of the sequencing of the issues. This is the rule that in criminal cases, the defendant must give evidence before other defence witnesses. However, since you will usually start with the defence theory of the case this should not be a problem(May (1990)).

There are many different ways in which a defence opening speech can be organised. According to Haddad (1979) a defence opening should include the following:

* an explanation of the procedure to be followed in the criminal trial and the jury's part in that process

* a statement of fundamental principles which protect defendants, for example, presumption of innocence, the concept of reasonable doubt, the fact that an indictment is not evidence of guilt

* a statement of the defence theory of the case; convey the 'not guilty' suggestion strongly

- a statement of what the defence believes it will prove in the case; be careful not to promise what you cannot prove

- a statement to acquaint the jury with the defendant personally. Humanise the defendant by referring to his employment, friendships, family and concerns. Interweave these details with factual evidence to create a living picture of the case and identification with the accused. Persuade the jury that the defendant is a good person; once juries make up their minds they rarely change them

At this stage of the trial, the prosecution evidence will have been presented and there may be weaknesses which can be drawn to the jury's attention. Here the value of keeping a note of the prosecution opening will become clear. Was there anything which the prosecution said it would prove in opening which they have failed to prove? If so, have they broken their promise to the jury? If so the jury should know that. It may be possible to weave your comments into the presentation of the defence theory of the case. Usually though the defence theory of the case should be stated clearly and unambiguously. This may be difficult if you are trying to integrate newly discovered facts. Consider the primacy effect; it might be better to offer the defence theory of the case first and then look at the prosecution evidence.

Much of what the defence might say depends on what has gone before; for example, whether or not the prosecution has already dealt fairly with matters in opening, such as the burden of proof. If so, you should consider showing how fair you are by giving the prosecution credit. For example:

'Mr Bumptious said that it is the prosecution's duty to present evidence which will prove Mr Innocent's guilt beyond any reasonable doubt. He was right to tell you that and he explained your duty clearly and fairly. I do not need to emphasise the point. Let us now look at the evidence Mr Bumptious has produced ...'

In the Rouse trial Mr Douglas Finnemore made a brief opening speech to suggest the 'improbability and inherent unlikeliness' of the prosecution case and to remind the jury of their obligation to ignore the newspaper speculation which had surrounded the case. He said this about circumstantial evidence:

> '... While circumstantial evidence can be extremely strong, so strong that its inferences make the case one of almost mathematical certainty, it might fall far, far short of that. It is so easy to draw wrong inferences that you must take every care. This danger is increased a thousandfold in a case like the present, which is quite unprecedented in that the deceased remains unknown and unidentified ...'

Again the significance of the primacy effect is a strong argument for proceeding as quickly as possible to establishing the defence theory of the case. Finnemore offered the jury a theory of the case based on an accident. He could be reasonably confident that the prosecution had not firmly established that the fire must have been planned. His remaining problem was Rouse's conduct during and after the fire. His explanation of this conduct was as follows:

> 'He had left the car and a few minutes later saw it in flames. He ran up to it, saw no sign of his companion, and all alone, at two in the morning, with no-one to help, became panic stricken and ran past his car shouting 'My God, My God!' His nerve broke. He ran away with one idea hammering away in his head; somehow to escape from the blazing horror in the road. Is it not a story strongly indicative of a man who has lost his nerve and ran away, and not in the least that of a man who was a cool and callous criminal?'

What devices does Finnemore use to stimulate the jury to focus on his theory of the case?

4.6   Structuring openings in civil cases

In civil cases the plaintiff generally offers evidence first and the defence follows. Apart from defamation, civil cases are usually tried by a judge alone. This obviously calls for some adjustment of the tactics which may be used in jury trials. The language may be logical, even legalistic, and the use of any psychological anchors should be more subtle. Remember, though, judges are human. Do not throw your basic presentation skills out of the window; a judge is there to be persuaded.

A conventional opening speech follows the introduction with a statement of the plaintiff's cause of action, an outline of the material facts and those facts which are in issue between the parties, an outline of the evidence and the relevant principles of law and a statement of why the plaintiff should succeed on the facts which will be proved.

It is important to outline the legal issues for the judge. Do not assume that the judge will automatically know everything about the case that you know. The judge will appreciate clarity and logic and a structure which assists her to organise the issues. It is noticeable that judges often start making notes at that point of the opening where the advocate outlines those things which need to be proved to establish the claim. For example:

'In proving this claim of misrepresentation I will show: first, that there was a pre-contractual statement of fact; second, that this was negligently made; third, that the plaintiff was intended to rely and did rely on this statement; and fourth, that he has suffered damage as a consequence'.

In ordering the facts attention should be paid to the order in which evidence will be called. This may be determined by the optimal organisation of the facts of the case (for example, chronological, topical or logical, see pages 60-61) or the order in which it is proposed to call witnesses. In a personal injury case, for example, this would frequently mean starting with the plaintiff and finishing with the medical expert. The defence can also choose a sequence for its witnesses for tactical reasons. If the defence believes that the plaintiff is a malingerer they may start with their own medical expert. If the defence can cast doubt on the plaintiff's lack of reliability in relation to his symptoms it may cast doubt on the rest of his evidence.

4.7 Summary

- organise your openings to reflect the order in which witnesses will appear
- remember the 'primacy' and 'recency' effects
- start with strong material
- speak to the jury
- interest the jury, in 'the story' and provide them with 'psychological anchors'
- anticipate weaknesses and confront them if necessary

4.8 End of chapter references and additional reading

Birkett N
(1948)
The Art of Advocacy
Character and Skills for the Trial Cases
American Bar Association Journal
Vol 34

Boon A
(1992)
Skills for legal functions II:
Representation and advice
Institute of Advanced Legal studies

Evans J
(1992)
Advocacy at the Bar: A Beginner's Guide
Blackstone Press

Haddad F E
(1979)
The Criminal Case: The Opening
Statement
Trial Vol 15 No 10

Julien A S
(1985)
Julien's Eight and a Half Rules
on Opening Statements
American Bar Association Journal Vol 71

Lindquist W I
(1982)
Advocacy in Opening Statements
Litigation Vol 8 No 3

May R
(1990)
Criminal Evidence
Ch 1
Sweet and Maxwell

Munkman J
(1991)
The Technique of Advocacy
Ch 9
Butterworth

Stone
(1992)
Stone's Justices' Manual
Vol 1
Butterworth
Shaw

Stein J E   *The Rhetorical Question and Other*
(1977)   *Forensic Speculations*
                             Litigation Vol 3 No 4

Vinson D E   *How to Persuade Jurors*
(1985)   American Bar Association Journal Vol 71

CHAPTER

5 Questioning

"A prosecution for reckless driving at Leicester Crown Court. The defendant is being examined about her speed.

'So you turned into Charles Street. How fast were you going?'

'Not more than 20 miles an hour.'

'What gear were you in?'

'Jeans and a T-shirt.' "

Berlins (1992)

5.1　Context

There are two situations in which the advocate asks questions; questioning his own witnesses and questioning the other side's witnesses. Examination-in-chief is where the advocate elicits evidence from his own witnesses. Cross-examination is the opportunity given to opposing counsels to ask questions about issues covered in examination-in-chief. A defendant in a criminal trial cannot be cross-examined unless she gives evidence in chief.

A basic rule for examining witnesses is that questions should be expressed in simple language, even where the witness is familiar with jargon. This is particularly the case where there is a jury. However, even where there is no jury other witnesses in court may need to be able to follow the evidence.

In questioning witnesses there are many different types of questions which can be asked.

5.2   Open and closed questions

On open and closed questions generally see 'Negotiation' by Diana Tribe and 'Interviewing & Counselling' by Jenny Chapman in this series.

There are different views about the use of open questions in examining witnesses. The consensus is that they should not be used in cross-examination because a witness should not be given a chance to explain his answers. In leading evidence from your own witnesses, however, some discretion may be exercised. A shy, nervous witness may appreciate closed questions which will help him to feel at ease in giving evidence. On other occasions an anxious witness may gain confidence in being allowed to respond more freely to early questions on personal details and immaterial matters. The advocate must judge which approach will help to get the best out of each witness.

If you have a witness who is very persuasive it may be advantageous to give him an opportunity to speak at length. This may arise with a witness of fact or an expert witness. Narrative is generally more convincing than the fragmented testimony produced by closed questions. The risk is that the witness may deal with irrelevant matters or present their information in an illogical sequence or in a way which is unfavourable to your case. The most serious risk in criminal trials is that prejudicial material may inadvertently come out, such as previous convictions. These disadvantages may be offset by the authenticity of the evidence. In any event a witness can be interrupted and refocused or, as in interviewing, asked to elaborate on some part of his response to an open question.

5.3   Hypothetical questions

Hypothetical questions are sometimes used to test the logical boundaries of a piece of evidence, for example:

Q: You have told me that you did not think it necessary to call an ambulance. Would you have called an ambulance if the plaintiff had hit her head?

5.4   Leading questions

Leading questions are questions which either, by their form, suggest the answer - for example 'You were in the shop that day, weren't you' - or which take for granted certain facts which the witness has not sworn to - for example 'What did the accused do in the shop?' - when the witness has not said that the accused was in the shop.

In questioning her own witnesses the advocate must avoid leading the witness on any issue which is, or which may be, material. Leading questions are forbidden for the following reasons:

- it is presumed any witness called by a party is potentially biased in favour of that party

- there is a risk that leading questions bring out only that evidence which is favourable to the questioner's client

- the likelihood of yes/ no answers means that witnesses may not express their full meaning in their own words

Denroche (1963-4)

Sometimes your own witness may be evasive or even refuse to answer questions. With the leave of the court leading questions can be put to a 'hostile witness' which the advocate has himself called to give evidence. The court must first decide that the witness' evidence is 'hostile' as opposed to unfavourable. Cross-examination of hostile witnesses must be limited to their evidence and should not touch on their character. However, such a witness may be confronted with contradictory evidence or inconsistent prior statements (Rules of the Supreme Court Order 38 Rule 1(3)). It is desirable to have a signed proof of evidence from the witness as the basis for discrediting the testimony.

Murphy and Barnard (1990)

5.5   Leading questions in cross-examination

Cross-examination is often based entirely on leading questions. This allows the advocate to put her own theory of the case to a witness with every question. The witness is forced to either accept the premise of the advocate's question or to correct it. Linguistic analysis of this process produces some interesting examples. Drew uses an example taken from a rape trial in the US in which counsel is questioning the victim about a meeting with the accused on an occasion before the alleged rape. In the original text different speech patterns are emphasised. These are omitted here. Instead, look at the questions and answers which are italicised. What can you deduce about the advocate's theory of the case? What is the significance of the questions and of the attempted corrections by the witness?

Q: And you went out to a *bar* in Boston, is that correct?

A: Its a *club*.

Q: Its where girls and fellas meet isn't it?

A: *People go* there.

Q: And during that evening, didn't Mr X come over *to sit with you?*

A: Sat at our table ...

Q: Well, didn't he ask you if, on that night, he *wanted you to be his girl?* ... Didn't he ask you that?

A: *I don't remember* what he said to me that night.

Q: Well, you had some *fairly lengthy conversations* with the defendant, didn't you? On that evening of February 14th?

A: Well, *we were all talking*.

At this point the advocate suggests that the accused had invited the witness out on that occasion. She replied that she did not remember.

Q: Well, you knew, at that time, that the defendant was interested in you, didn't you?

A: *He asked me how I'd been*, just stuff like that.

Q: Just asked how you'd been; but he kissed you goodnight. Is that right?

A Yeah, he asked me if he could.

Q: He asked if he *could*? ...

Drew (1990)

5.6   A sequence of three questions

The use of a three part list can be used to emphasise a line of questions. Witnesses will often agree to the first two points on the list but realise that agreement with the third point symbolises completeness. In this extract, again from Drew, the witness is a co-defendant, with her daughter, on a charge of possessing heroin. Here she is describing how her daughter had previously been in trouble with the police.

Q: What kind of trouble?

A: She was found with some works in her pocket.

Q: Works eh? Now where did you pick up the slang expression 'works'?

A: I've heard it used quite frequently.

Q: What's meant by the term 'works'?

A: It means uh, a needle.

Q: A syringe?

A: Yes sir.

Q: A cooker?

A: Ye - I don't know about the cooker.

Q: Pardon?

A: I don't know about the cooker.

Drew (1990)

The point that Drew makes is that we have a strong reaction that three is a complete list. A list of two items may have common properties. However, it is only when the list reaches three that it is possible to generalise those common properties. To acknowledge familiarity with three drug terms would imply greater knowledge of the language of drug addicts than it would be wise to admit.

5.7   Probing, insinuating and confrontational questions

In 'The Technique of Advocacy', Munkman identifies three kinds of questions which are typically used in cross-examination; probing, insinuating and confrontational questions. He describes a strategy which uses these questioning techniques which he calls 'undermining'.

> 'Its object is not to break down the evidence by inquiring into the facts, but to take away the foundations of the evidence by showing that either i) the witness does not know what he is talking about, or ii) if he does know the truth, he cannot be trusted to tell it.'

Munkman (1991)

Probing questions are often used to gather further details of a witness' account and to test that account against other facts. They introduce into evidence an account to which the witness is committed. Often these questions cover matters which seem inconsequential. However, they help to create a picture which may or may not be coherent.

A witness who is telling lies will have needed to carefully think through his or her story. It is often difficult to anticipate all the surrounding detail which may be required. A witness account may therefore be richer in texture where it is truthful than where it is false. That is why witnesses who agree to lie are sensible if they transpose an experience they have in common to the day in question. The alibi of the accused may be that he went to the dogs with Lefty. Lefty and the accused agree that they will describe the visit on the previous Friday since the detail on which they can be tested will correspond. However, anticipating this, the prosecution will check what the weather was like on the second Friday, which dogs were running, who else was there etc as material for cross-examination. Another rule-of-thumb for spotting true accounts is that they often have ambiguities or inconsistencies. The truthful witness acknowledges these and will not fill the gap. A false account often points consistently one way.

If you believe a witness is lying probing questions force him to invent more lies. The more such detail the witness gives, the greater the risk of contradiction in later answers. The detail he gives can also be compared with similar detail provided by witnesses with whom they may have 'agreed a story'. While the main points of a story can be rehearsed the detail may be shaky. Probing questions can also be used to disguise the main point of a series of questions.

Take this example of an imaginary cross-examination. The witness claims to have seen John Doe at the Purple Parrot club before midnight. The advocate's ultimate aim is to show that the witness is mistaken or lying. He knows that at some point in the evening the witness asked where John Doe was:

Q: Why did you go to the Purple Parrot?

A: The pubs had closed and I wanted a drink.

Q: You were in the Goose and Turkey?

A: Yes.

Q: You telephoned your wife at 11.30 from the Goose and Turkey?

A: Well, more like 11.25.

Q: You would accept that the doors of The Goose and Turkey were closed at 11.30 and that the landlord, while locking up, asked you to finish your telephone call and leave?

A: If that's what he says.

Q: How soon after that did you go to the Purple Parrot?

A: Straight away.

Q: How did you get there?

A: I walked.

Q: At what time did you see John Doe at the Purple Parrot?

A: Around 11.45.

Insinuating questions are used to put an alternative version of events, that is your version, to a witness. The questions to the alleged rape victim (see the dialogue above) fall into this category. Insinuating questions may be subtle, for example

Q: When you arrived at the Purple Parrot you brought Richard Roe a drink, didn't you?

A: Yes.

Q: You were talking at the bar?

A: Yes.

Q: Did you say to Richard Roe 'Have you seen that welsher Doe'?

A: I may have said something like that.

Q: That was after midnight?

A: No, that must have been around 11.45.

Q: Would you accept that it takes 20 minutes to walk from the Goose and Turkey to the Purple Parrot?

A: Possibly.

Q: You were talking to a woman at the bar for 15 minutes before speaking to Richard Roe?

A: I had a few words.

Q: And then you were talking to Richard Roe for at least ten minutes before you mentioned John Doe?

A: Well, I think I probably mentioned him quicker than that.

Q: Do you think that it must have been later than 11.45 that you asked Richard Roe about John Doe?

Insinuating questions can be stronger than this. There may be a point where you cannot make further progress with the witness. Here, insinuating questions allow you to put your case to the witness. In all probability the witness will answer 'no' to the question; that does not matter. If you are going to challenge a witness' account in your closing speech the witness must have had a chance to deal with your alternative. The insinuating question is an effective way of doing this, particularly when it is used as a series of questions, using the 'inevitable conclusion' sequence:

Q: You arrived at the Purple Parrot at 11.50 at the earliest didn't you?

A: No.

Q: You then spent at least 25 minutes in conversation with various people in the club, including the woman at the bar and Richard Roe, didn't you?

A: No.

Q: You asked Richard Roe if he had seen John Doe well after midnight, didn't you?

A: No, it was before midnight.

Q: In fact, you did not see John Doe at the Purple Parrot at all that night, did you?

A: Yes, I did.

Confrontational questions present the witness with a fact which they cannot deny, because it has been proved or will be proved by other evidence; for example 'you signed a statement at the police station?' or 'The Goose and Turkey was locked up at 11.30?' As Munkman says, 'Confrontation is only firm insinuation on a massive scale' In some instances the witness can be confronted in strong terms, depending on the strength of the evidence you have. For example:

Q: You have been paid £3,000 by Mr Big to lie about John Doe being at the Purple Parrot that night, haven't you?

A: Its a lie, I swear to God!

5.8   Ridicule, repetition and rivetting

In 'The Art of the Advocate', Richard Du Cann suggests three additional techniques which may be used in cross-examination. He calls these the 'three Rs'; ridicule, repetition and rivetting.

Ridicule might be used to emphasise the inherent unlikelihood of an answer given in cross examination. For example:

Q: You spent four hours at the Goose and Turkey drinking and you say you ran to the Purple Parrot?

A: The drinks are cheaper at the Purple Parrot before midnight.

Q: You needed a drink?

Repetition of a question may emphasise that the witness' answer is evasive:

Q: Why did Mr Big give you a cheque for £3,000?

A: I did some jobs for him.

Q: What were the jobs which you did for this £3,000?

A: This and that.

Q: What were the jobs?

A: I can't remember exactly; it was a while ago.

Q: This is a simple question; what were the jobs which you did for Mr Big for which you received £3,000?

The other purpose of repeating questions, according to Du Cann, is the hope that the witness will use the same form of words in response. This suggests that the witness may have rehearsed answers to difficult questions. This is more likely to be effective if the question is returned to after probing the answer first.

'Rivetting' is securing the witness' commitment to a particular story. It is particularly effective where the witness has elaborated a lie in response to probing questions; this prevents the witness backtracking. Say, for example, that Mr Big has already told the court that the witness decorated his Kensington flat in January. Having hooked the witness the advocate can easily let him slip.

Q: The decorating you did for Mr Big, where was that?

A: It was his house in Newham.

Q: Ah ... Now then, Mr Big has already told the court that it was his Kensington flat! Now you say it was a house in Newham?

A: I'm sorry; I thought you meant the decorating I did last year. This year it was the Kensington flat.

Follow-up probing questions can prevent the witness from wriggling off the hook:

Q: Did you paint the Newham House inside and out?

A: Yes.

Q: How did you get there from Clapham?

A: I drove my van up.

Q: This was in about January this year?

A: Yes.

Q: Was the weather fine for painting outside in January?

A: There were enough good days.

Q: Did you also wallpaper inside?

A: I did.

Q: What wallpaper did you use downstairs?

A: There was a green pattern in the lounge and a plain paper in the dining room.

Q: And upstairs, what did you use in the bedrooms?

A: Well, those were painted.

Q: How many floors does the Newham house have?

A: Three floors I think.

Q: Did you paint the third floor also? ...

The witness is now firmly rivetted to his position; he painted a house in Newham this January. He cannot say that it was a flat in Kensington.

5.9   Enlivening testimony

Your aim in presenting your own evidence is that it should be complete, coherent, convincing and as interesting as possible. Avoid long or confusing questions and repetitious questioning of different witnesses; aim for simplicity and brevity. Save the detail for where it matters, in the action part of the testimony, not the background. Aim for vivid description and engagement of the witness. Avoid using terms which sound unconvincing or pompous. Common examples of terms to avoid, particularly when using insinuating or confrontational questions, are 'I put it to you that ...' or 'I suggest to you that ...'

There are many ways of changing the pattern of questions like, for example, a change of tense:

Q: What did you do then?

A: I got out the car and waited.

Q: Now you are standing by the car, tell us what you see ...

5.10   Pitfalls

Avoid preparing a list of questions. There is a risk that unexpected answers will cause you to lose your flow. You may even find yourself being more concerned about the next question than the answers. Some questions may need to be carefully structured, for example, technical questions put to experts.This forethought will hopefully avoid the embarrassment of being corrected by an expert. If you put a hypothetical question to an expert this needs to be carefully thought out in advance.

It is often said that an advocate should never ask questions he does not know answers to. This is certainly true when asking questions of your own witness. It is also a fine general principle in cross-examination. However, only rarely will you know what the other side's witness is going to say. It is sometimes difficult to make progress with a witness without a calculated gamble or two. You should not ask a witness who has made a damaging point against you the reasons behind the answer. Their explanation may make their answer even more compelling. Ask questions which gradually develop the evidence you wish to come out. If your questions are carefully framed you can often adopt a different tack before the point where an unfavourable response would disastrous. Younger argues that there are two instances in which the advocate may break this 'Golden Rule'

> '... Even though he does not know the answers a good cross-examiner may ask a question when he does not care what the answer is. Second, it is possible not to know the answer to a particular question at the start of the cross-examination, but to discover the answer by cunning use of preliminary questions to which the answer is either known or unimportant. The advocate closes doors, he eliminates possible explanations, and gradually escalates himself to the point where he does know the answer. He has learned it in the course of cross-examination and, so, he may now ask the question'.
>
> Younger (1977)

When you have got what you want from a witness, leave that line of questioning. Avoid the temptation of ramming home the point. The question intended to be the 'final nail in the coffin' all too often provides an opportunity to the witness to explain away a slip they have made. If you fear that the court has not seen the significance of a point you can emphasise it in your closing speech. It is for the other advocate to decide whether to try to repair any damage in re-examination.

5.11   Examination-in-chief

So far this Chapter has concentrated on questioning techniques in cross-examination. Other special considerations apply to questioning strategies in examination-in-chief. In examination-in-chief the objective is to present your evidence so that it is clearly understood and persuasive.

> 'Direct examination is more important than cross-examination, the opening statement or closing argument. For unless the outlook is so dismal that the only hope in litigation is to create confusion, a coherent statement of the facts by the witnesses is essential to the jury's understanding and acceptance of your position ...'

> McElhaney (1976)

One aspect of the new rules on exchange of witness statements (see 'Planning' Chapter Three at para 3.2.1) is that the court may order that statements exchanged stand as evidence in chief. Obviously this may diminish the role of examination-in-chief in civil matters and make the task of preparing witness statements even more important.

5.12   Organisation

A chronological order is often the most appealing way of outlining facts. However, chronology may sometimes be more confusing than other sequences (logical, topical or 'inevitable conclusion' see also Chapter Three at para 3.6). Some cases may require a mixture of different approaches. In examination-in-chief a combination of chronological and topical is often best. Events which dominate are often recalled first; we then tend to put events into a chronological context.

This combined approach requires each important event to be approached separately. The topic is signalled to the witness and the court and the main elements brought out; the questioner then returns to the chronological order. The stock in trade questions of examination in chief are typically the 'W' questions; these help the advocate to ask non-leading questions. For example:

'*Wh*ere did he go?'

'*Wh*at did he say then?'

'*Wh*o else was there?'

'*Wh*en did you arrive?'

'*Wh*y did you go there?' and possibly

'Can you show us?'

Pace and flow of questioning needs to be kept up. This helps to keep up the response rate of witnesses and adds to authority of answers. It also sustains the interest of the audience. Some advocates use links which give them time to think, for example, 'Let me ask you this ...' Try to avoid these and instead pause if you must; you will probably find that, without the crutch of these devices, you will speed up.

Do not repeat every answer the witness gives. It may ensure that an answer is not missed but, if done too often, it loses impact. If you immediately repeat an answer there is an additional risk that the witness will qualify what she said. An answer which you particularly want to be emphasised can be included in a later question. For example:

Q: Mr A, you have already told me that you noticed the goods in the defendant's basket as she left the shop. Can you tell me precisely where you were standing at that moment?

Avoid asking your witnesses to comment on areas they are not familiar with. Remember that you cannot challenge your own witness on prior inconsistent statements unless the court is prepared to declare that witness hostile. Do not ask too many questions. Their uncertainty on any issue may weaken the impact of the rest of their evidence or give the other advocate material for cross-examination. The more questions you ask the more likely you are to find an issue on which the witness is uncertain.

5.13 Leading questions in examination-in-chief

In examination-in-chief leading questions may be used only in relation to preliminary details (name address etc), areas agreed between the advocates or on points which are not in issue (see the County Court Practice notes to Order 20 Rule 4). The leave of the court may be given 'so far as justice may require' (Rules of the Supreme Court Order 38 Rule 1(3)) for example for very young or old witnesses.

So an opening sequence, using permissible leading questions, may be as follows:

Q: Your name is Red Ridinghood?

A: Yes.

Q: And you live at Edge of the Forest Cottage at Woodleigh?

A: Yes.

Q: You attend Woodleigh Comprehensive School?

A: Yes.

Q: On 1st June last year you were taking some groceries to your grandma?

A: Yes, I was.

Q: Where does your grandma live?

A: At Centre Cottage, in the middle of the forest.

Q: Did you meet anybody on this journey?

A: Yes, I met a wolf.

Note that the advocate may guide the witness by the form of question. The question about grandma's house is a transition from leading to guiding questions before the advocate arrives at potentially contentious issues.

An open question now would be:

Q: Could you describe this wolf?

However, you may wish to be more specific. If, for example, you know that the defendant habitually wears a distinctive collar, you could say:

Q: What was the wolf wearing?

A: He wore a collar.

Q: Could you describe this collar?

You may also guide the witness:

Q: What colour was the wolf's fur?

It is acceptable to indicate the issue which is of interest or to offer questions with a limited range of answers where nothing turns on the answer, for example, 'Did you speak to Mr X at work on the 14th February?'. However, there are advantages in allowing the witness to give their own evidence when this enhances of the credibility of what is said. For example:

Q: Did you speak to Mr X again after the January incident?

A: Yes.

Q: When was that?

A: Sometime in February.

Q: Can you remember the exact date?

A: I think it was around the 14th.

Q: Where did this conversation take place?

A: At work.

It is the opposing advocate's responsibility to object to inappropriate leading questions immediately, preferably before an answer is given. Sometimes the judge will intervene to warn the questioning advocate against the use of inappropriate leading questions. It is important to master the art of asking questions which do not lead in examination-in-chief:

'if you so conduct your examination in chief that your opponent must sit still, that is a very great triumph; but if you so conduct yourself that you give your opponent the opportunity of protesting against leading questions or other irregularities your influence begins to go, your control over the jury begins to vanish'.

Birkett (1948)

Remember that when you have finished examining a witness the other advocate may wish to cross-examine. The judge may even have a question. You should always indicate that you have finished by saying 'I have no further questions, Your Honour'. You should also indicate to the witness that he should remain where he is. If the other advocate does not wish to cross-examine you may wish to ask if the witness can be released. This can be particularly important with expert witnesses for whose services your client must pay a professional fee.

5.14   Introducing real evidence

In criminal law real evidence is a document (eg a fraudulent cheque) as opposed, for example, to a document admitted in evidence under s 23 or s 24 of the Criminal Justice Act (1988) (such as a statement of a deceased person or a document created or received in the course of trade) or object which may need to be put in as an exhibit at a trial. Real evidence will need to be identified by witnesses before it is admitted as evidence. There must be a foundation in the evidence for the admission of such items. The main requirement is that they must be relevant to the issues in the case, but there are also a number of exclusionary rules covering, for example, hearsay (See May (1990) especially 1-20 to 1-26)

Alternatively in a civil case, for example in a personal injury case where the plaintiff may have expenses which are not agreed, the undisputed supporting documentary evidence might be introduced as follows:

Q: Mr Plaintiff, did you have any other expenses as a result of this accident?

A: I did.

Q: Could you tell the court what these were?

A: Yes. I had to attend the hospital for physiotherapy and went there by taxi.

Q: Did you keep any record of these visits?

A: I always asked the taxi driver for a receipt.

Q: Will you look at the bundle which the usher will hand to you?

A: Yes.

Q: Are those the receipts you collected for taxi fares to and from the hospital for your physiotherapy?

A: They are.

Advocate: Your honour, this will be plaintiff's exhibit P6.

When evidence is disputed the introduction of real evidence will be more formal. The other side, forewarned that you wish to put the evidence in, may wish the jury to retire while the judge hears the argument. Such evidence may need to be presented to a witness before it is received in evidence (Stone's Justices' Manual (1992)). In these cases the full procedure would be as follows:

- request that exhibit be marked for identification. For example, 'I request this be marked as a defence exhibit for identification'

- lay the foundation for admitting exhibit. It is important to remember the primary criteria of relevance and admissibility (Stone's Justices' Manual ibid). If a photograph, for example, ask the photographer where and when the photograph was taken, and have him confirm that the negative has not been tampered with. An identifying mark should then be put on by the clerk

- allow opposing counsel to examine exhibit

- offer exhibit into evidence. 'Defence exhibit 14 for identification is offered in evidence'

- give the exhibit to the trial judge for inspection

- possible voire dire examination of witness by opposing counsel on issue of admissibility
- ruling on admissibility
- testimony concerning exhibit
- give the jury exhibit or copy

Note that in civil law the definition of real evidence is limited to 'material objects other than documents' (see O'Hare & Hill on Civil Litigation (1990)).

5.15   Anticipating cross-examination

There is much to be said for having your own witnesses deal with potentially embarrassing issues in examination-in-chief. It shows that you are prepared to be open about difficulties, it can draw the sting of the questioning which will follow in cross-examination and it will give your witness an opportunity to put the best light on events.

> 'It is usually advisable to anticipate what the opposition is going to try and do to your witnesses and do it yourself before the other side gets the chance. In other words to try to steal the thunder of the opposition; bring out the weak points in your case as soon as possible and in your own way rather than try to explain them away later.'

> McElhaney (1978)

However, you need to be careful not to undermine the impact of your evidence or to open up an area which, while presenting difficulties for your case, may have been inaccessible to the other advocate without your lead. Questions to ask yourself are, 'is it inevitable that this witness will be cross-examined on this point and, if so, is it necessary that I prepare the ground in examination-in-chief? If I leave this question and the other side raises this question will it reflect badly on them?' If the problem must be tackled you can confront your own witness with the difficult point and seek an explanation. In your demeanour and by your follow-up questions show that you accept the witness's explanation.

For example, in the Rouse case, Finnemore, tried to give Rouse the opportunity to explain his conduct after he left the incident in Hardingstone Lane and the lies which he had told during the period before his arrest. How successful was this attempt? Could Finnemore have phrased his questions any differently in order to help Rouse put the best face on his actions?

Q: Do you remember giving some explanation of why you did not have the car?

A: I gave some explanation; what it was I really could not say.

Q: Was it a truthful one?

A: No, I could not say that very well because it was very lengthy and long. Another thing too, there were ladies present, and one would hardly give the whole details in any case.

Q: Were you going to tell about the car?

A: I had not thought about that. They would have to know eventually.

What is the potential for cross-examination on these answers?

5.16 Summary

- keep questions simple and short
- use 'open ended' questions with great caution
- keep leading questions mainly for cross-examination
- use probing questions to elicit a witness' commitment to 'a story'
- use insinuating questions to put your own theory of the case to the other side's witness
- use confronting questions only when you can prove your point
- do not repeat answers

5.17   End of chapter references and additional reading

Archbold M I   *Archbold Pleadings, Evidence and*
(1993)   *Practice in Criminal Cases*
                       Vol 1 Ch 8
                       Sweet & Maxwell

Berlins M   Guardian Sept 30
(1992)

Birkett N   *The Art of Advocacy: Character and*
(1948)   *Skills for the Trial Cases*
                       American Bar Association Journal Vol 34

Denroche S G   *Leading Questions*
(1963-4)   Criminal Law Quarterly

Drew P   *Language in the Judicial Process*
(1990)   Plenum Press

May R   Criminal Evidence
(1990)   Sweet and Maxwell

McElhaney J W   *An Introduction to Direct Examination*
(1976)   Litigation Vol 2 No 2

McElhaney J W   *Rehabilitation*
(1978)   Litigation Vol 4 No 4

Munkman J   *The Technique of Advocacy*
(1991)   Ch 2
                       Butterworth

Murphy P and   *Evidence and Advocacy*
Barnard D   Ch 9
(1990)   Blackstone Press

Murphy P   *A Practical Approach to Evidence*
(1992)   Ch 13
                       Blackstone Press

O'Hare and Hill (1990)	*Civil Litigation* Longman
Stone (1992)	*Stones' Justices' Manual* Vol 3 Butterworth Shaw
Younger I (1977)	*A Letter in which Cicero lays down the Ten Commandments of Cross Examination* Litigation Vol 3 No 2
Zuckerman A A S (1989)	*The Principles of Criminal Evidence* Ch 7 Clarendon Press

CHAPTER

6 Cross-examination

> '... In the case of one who will not speak the truth unless
> against his will, the greatest happiness in an examiner is
> to extort from him what he does not wish to say; and this
> cannot be done otherwise than by questions which seem
> wide of the matter in hand; for to these he will give such
> answers as he thinks will not hurt his party; and then
> from various particulars which he may confess, he will be
> reduced to the inability of denying what he does not wish
> to acknowledge ...'

Quintillian 'Institutes of Oratory'

6.1 Aims

'Cross-examination is the process whereby a party seeks: (a) to
test the veracity and accuracy of evidence in chief, given by a
witness called for another party; and (b) to elicit from that witness
any relevant facts which may be favourable to the cross-
examiner. Cross-examination designed solely to discredit the
witness and to destroy or reduce his credibility, is sometimes
known as 'impeachment' and is perfectly permissible.'

Murphy (1992)

(and see County Court Practice: notes to Order 20 Rule 4)

According to Archbold (1993),

'The credibility of a witness depends upon: (1) his knowledge of
the facts to which he testifies; (2) his disinterestedness; (3) his
integrity; (4) his veracity and (5) his being bound to speak the
truth by such as he deems obligatory ... The degree of credit his
testimony deserves will be in proportion to the jury's assessment
of these qualities.'

The advocate aims to have his own evidence accepted and
that of the other side rejected. A secondary aim of cross-

examination is to put your client's case to the other side's witnesses through the use of insinuating questions. The court is there to evaluate the evidence for both sides and to make a finding of fact; this cannot be done unless the evidence has been tested.

6.2 Organisation

Organisation of your cross-examination will depend on many strategic decisions you make in your planning. In general, as with opening speeches, you will probably find a topical arrangement within a chronological framework satisfactory for most purposes. Your specific approach may only be confirmed during examination-in-chief and you therefore need to build some flexibility into your plans.

If you decide that you must attack the credibility of the witness you can attack credibility generally or only in relation to specific testimony. If you are attacking the witness' general credibility (for example, his character) you may choose to confront the witness at the start of cross-examination if your evidence is strong. You may choose to delay until you see how the witness performs if your evidence is weak. If you are attacking credibility in relation to the witness' recollection of certain incidents only you will organise your attack according to topic area (see, for example, Archbold (1993) especially 8-141 to 8-200).

As you evaluate a witness in examination-in-chief you may think that he is prepared to make concessions. You will wish to organise to maximise the effect of these concessions and also try to ensure that beneficial testimony is not damaged by attacks on credibility. When you are trying to 'rivet' a witness into their position (see Chapter 5), close all escape routes by using probing questions before moving to insinuating or confronting questions. You should try to conceal the point of this kind of questioning for as long as possible.

Younger (1977)

6.3   Style

It is important that you retain self control. Do not quarrel with the witness and try to avoid commenting on any answer you are given. If you comment to try and highlight a point you will alert the witness to its significance and may lose your flow. You will have the opportunity to comment on the evidence in your final speech. Rarely would you allow a witness to explain or repeat evidence from examination-in-chief. If it was favourable evidence you can only lose by trying to have the witness embellish it.

Your use of leading questions will give you control of the witness. If he should go beyond the narrow questions you ask you can stop the witness. The judge will support your right to conduct your cross-examination as you see fit. However, she will not usually intervene unless she sees that you are not content with the way the witness answers your questions. It is unwise to appeal to the judge to control the witness since you may be seen to want support in a battle you are losing.

If you observe from examination-in-chief that you have a loquacious witness, you may try and strike a bargain.

> 'Mr Wolf, I am going to ask some questions about your evidence.
> I noticed that your answers to Mr Bumptious' questions where
> very full. Most of my questions you will be able to respond to with
> a simple 'yes' or 'no'. I hope you understand if I ask you to restrict
> yourself to a yes/no answer?'

The witness can do little else but agree. If he agrees but does not comply you can remind him of the bargain. If you have a witness who persistently and unhelpfully rambles on it is best to have a prepared speech, such as:

- 'Please stop there Mr Wolf; could you just answer the question I am asking. If I could remind you, the question I asked was ...'

If the problem continues,

- 'Mr Wolf, I have asked you once to answer the questions which I put to you. A simple 'yes' or 'no' will 'do'. If I could repeat the question ...'

Notice that these formulae do not require any response from the witness. You are less likely to get into an argument. A witness may sometimes protest that it is impossible to answer every question with a simple 'yes' or a 'no'.

Your response might be:

- 'Nevertheless, Mr Wolf, you will understand that I am here to ask questions; your role is to answer the questions I ask. Everyone in this court will be very grateful if we both do what is expected of us.'

When you cross-examine your questions should be clearly understood by everyone in court. Be economical in your questioning. Try to use short questions and plain words. Rather than:

- 'For what period of time did you maintain surveillance over the subject in question?'

Ask instead:

- 'How long did you watch him?'

Cross-examination should be as brief as is necessary to achieve your aims; a short cross-examination is more likely to make an impact on the memory. Seek only that information which will support your theory of the case; do not cross-examine every witness on every issue. Advocates sometimes believe that they can win a case by cross-examining; they stagger on, in a losing battle, looking for the 'killer punch'.

> 'Daily experience in criminal courts - especially in summary trials - shows that, apart from exceptional cases, an advocate should not normally expect to win by one brilliant coup in cross-examination. An exaggerated view of what can be achieved may induce an advocate to cross-examine, or to go on with it for too long, where this is unnecessary, dangerous or actually harmful to his case. A realistic view will enhance his performance.'

Stone (1988)

An overlong attempt to breakdown a witness may suggest anxiety on your part that the witness' evidence-in-chief was damaging. If you must conduct a long cross-examination you need good organisation and narrative sense so that the evidence is easily followed and its significance appreciated.

An advocate must be free to engage with the witness. Again, prepared questions may prevent this.

> 'Ideally an examination should be in the form of a 'spontaneous conversation'. This cannot be done if the advocate's head is buried in his brief.'

> Du Cann (1980)

A list of key topics, or a mind map, allows you to be flexible. This allows you to listen to the witness' responses. Witnesses sometimes make amazing admissions and contradict themselves, but advocates appear not to hear. Why? Rather than listening to the response they are anxiously looking for next question on their list. Edward Carson was nominated by Sir Norman Birkett 'the finest cross-examiner within my recollection at the English Bar'. He cites this example of Carson's quick thinking:

Q: Do you drink?

A: That is my business.

Q: Do you have any other?

That kind of riposte is made possible by careful attention to what the witness says.

6.4 Strategy

The first strategic issue in cross-examination is whether or not there is a need to cross-examine. If the witness is telling the truth as they see it the arguments for cross-examination are reduced. Do not feel that you must cross-examine every witness. It follows that cross-examination does not need to last for any particular period of time. You should look at a witness' evidence and decide precisely what the realistic objectives of cross-examination are; cross-examine efficiently to achieve those objectives and do no more than is necessary for that purpose.

Effective use of cross-examination is enhanced by understanding some basic premises about how people act. Most people tell as much of the truth, as they see it, as they can. Skilled liars realise that the fewer lies they tell the easier it is to manage and protect their position. They are also able to lie convincingly while showing no physical signs of doing so. Others may appear untruthful when telling the truth; this appearance may be due to no more than anxiety or stress. For these reasons it would be rare for a witness' non-verbal responses to be commented upon by the advocate. This is a part of the advocate's responsibility to be fair to witnesses.

Nevertheless, the advocate will be aware of what impact the witness is having, particularly on a jury, and may need to adjust her questioning strategy accordingly. The advocate's detection of a lie can be put to the witness. This tactic must be exercised with the utmost caution; do not evoke sympathy for the witness by an unjustified accusation of lying. The main advantage of detecting a lie is in the potential for cross-examination on the point even if its significance may not be immediately apparent; people do not lie in court without good reason.

Most witnesses come to believe in the truth of the side for which they testify. Recollection and retelling are influenced by the fact that, being called by one side or the other, they have 'taken sides'. You may find that a witness called by the other side is unexpectedly favourable to you. While you can ask such a witness leading questions consider whether this is necessary. The weight of the evidence given may be enhanced if it is seen to be given freely and not under the pressure of leading questions.

The credibility of oral testimony depends on the apparent truthfulness of the witness and the plausibility of what they say; one without the other does not produce credible evidence. In assessing witnesses a judge or jury will affected by their own prejudices; they may be more affected by a witness' social standing or office than by what they say. People of 'good character' sometimes lie for what they believe to be good reasons. What is within the experience of one juror might seem incredible to another. What a witness says must be compared with other evidence or known facts. Although responses to questions are often misleading both the answers and the witness' demeanour will affect his credibility.

In dealing with witnesses advocates can adopt a friendly or a hostile demeanour. Friendliness may be appropriate where it is believed that the witnesses is honest but mistaken, hostility where they are believed to be lying. The benefits of adopting one of these demeanours lies in conveying the advocate's attitude to the particular witness to the court; treating all witnesses with hostility diminishes impact. There may be occasions where guile may be successful in trapping a witness who is lying.

> 'He worked with the precision of a surgeon - just the right pressure, with perfect timing, knowing when to push and when to withdraw. But he was also the actor - looking significantly at the jury after a point had been made, rocking back on his heels, then turning back to confront the witness, eyebrows raised over half moon spectacles, expressions of both satisfaction and scepticism to order.'

Hain (1976)

Hostility by the cross-examiner may backfire because there may be sympathy for a witness who appears to be hounded by the advocate; there may even be animosity towards the lawyer who is hostile. As a defensive reaction the witness may become even more committed to the testimony they have already given; has hostility ever persuaded you to change your mind? Hostility may be perceived as unreasonableness. Instead, you can show your disbelief by more subtle means.

Munkman observes that effective cross-examination alternates between the three main types of question.

'A probing question may be followed by a gentle insinuation and that in turn by a sudden pounce of firm insinuation.'

Constructive cross-examination attempts to build on those points where the witness can be persuaded to agree with your case. If a medical expert, for example, differs on causation, can she at least agree that your client's condition is painful?

See also para 6.7 below for some examples of choice of strategy in cross-examination.

6.5   Duties of the advocate in cross-examination

Richard Du Cann observes that the power given to an advocate in cross-examination is great. The advocate asks questions of the witness, can demand answers and choose the ground on which to fight having seen most the evidence. This power should not be seen to be abused.

In criminal cases the prosecutor has an obligation to establish the truth and not just to secure a guilty verdict. The accused cannot be asked about previous convictions. He loses this 'shield' if he gives evidence of his own good character or attacks the character of a prosecution witness. However, when acting as a prosecutor the advocate should not merely put on a 'neutral' cap. She remains under an obligation to convince the jury. As we have seen this may require her to show conviction and determination. On the other hand, the defence in criminal cases has no general obligation to establish 'the truth'.

In criminal trials both prosecution and defence should not allow witnesses to go beyond answering the question; their response may not be treated as evidence and if they reveal certain information (such as the accused's convictions) there may be a mis-trial. In civil cases either side may call evidence to establish the 'general reputation' for untruthfulness of a witness.

Du Cann (1980)
Stone (1988)

6.6   Relating oral evidence to previous statements

You should be aware of the contents of all previous statements made by witnesses and test oral evidence against such statements. One of the key cross-examination tools is evidential contradiction, usually in relation to previous statements. Clearly, it is of great benefit to the advocate to show that a witness for the other side has not told the truth in some material respect. Sometimes the opportunity to expose contradiction will offer itself unexpectedly. In this case the advocate should expose the contradiction and should succeed in damaging the credibility of the witness.

In the excerpt from the Rouse trial below, Birkett was cross-examining Rouse on the statement he had made to the police that he felt 'responsible' for the death of the man in his car. There are two things to note in this passage. First, the use that Birkett makes of the fact that the police constable was not challenged on the substance of the statement Rouse gave. Second, towards the end of the passage Birkett demands an answer to a question which he thinks the witness is evading.

Q: You never did anything to try and help when the car was burning?

A: I could not see if he was there for one thing.

Q: Do you swear that?

A: I swear that.

Q: Did you say in the first explanation you made 'I saw the man was inside and tried to open the door'?

A: I cannot say that; I do not remember saying it.

Q: Detective-Sergeant Skelly in this court gave evidence, and it was not cross-examined on, that you said, right at the outset ... 'I saw the man was inside and tried to open the door, but I could not, as the car was then a mass of flames'.

Q: Was that true?

A: I did not go within several feet of the fire. I went towards the opening of the door.

Q: Was that true?

A: No it was not exactly true; it was not true at all. I did not see the man.

6.7   A choice of strategies for cross-examination

Some examples.

In the Rouse trial much of Birkett's cross-examination was aimed at demonstrating the implausibility of Rouse's story. What device does Birkett use, in the following extract, to underline his message?

Q: You ran from fifteen yards past the car, where you had been, down towards the main road, and then turned back to pick up your case?

A: I did not go as far as the main road - only to there.

Q: But towards the main road, and then turned back to pick up your case?

A: Yes, two or three yards past the case.

Q: It was fortunate you remembered your case in your panic?

A: Yes. I believe I must have seen it.

Q: But your panic was not so great you could not stop and pick up your case?

A: Well, I think I saw it, to be quite frank.

One of the key limbs of the prosecution hypothesis in the Rouse case was that this fire could not have started accidentally. It must be remembered that the evidence was that the flames from the car were fifteen feet high. Colonel Cuthbert Buckle, a fire loss assessor and prosecution expert, gave evidence that there had been an intense fire under the bonnet; a continuous fire fed over a period of time certainly from the front of the car. Some of the brass parts at the front of the car were fused; this would require a heat of 1850°F applied for some time. Buckle found that the pipe which carried petrol from the petrol tank to the carburettor was loose by one whole turn of the nut. He loosened the same joint in another car by the same amount; he found that the leak created produced half a pint of petrol in one minute and 20 seconds.

Was Rouse able to contrive a fire of this intensity and duration? Did he know how to create a leak in the car's petrol system in order to feed the fire for a period of time? Before tackling Rouse on the cause of the fire, Birkett had to first deny him the escape route of ignorance. Did Rouse immediately spot the danger in Birkett's line of questioning? Did he attempt to evade the questions designed to establish his technical capability? What are the three stages of this line of questioning?

Q: You know a good deal about cars?

A: I have had a good many cars.

Q: How many?

A: I should not like to say - quite a number.

Q: Different makes?

A: Yes - I have had two Fords, two Overlands - several cars - two Morris Minors.

Q: Have you a garage?

A: Yes; I built it myself.

Q: With a working bench?

A: I should not quite give it that elaborate name. I use it as a bench, but it is only a little slab of wood.

Q: Where do you do the working repairs?

A: Yes, I do repairs; but it was not a bench; only a slab of wood.

Q: Where you do the working repairs. You have a fair working knowledge of cars?

A: Yes, I think so; a fair working knowledge.

Q: You know all about the engine, and the petrol supply and all the rest of it?

A: Yes.

Birkett has establish that Rouse 'knows all about cars'. He then moves to the issue of the petrol pipe with the loose nut.

Q: You know the union joint that has been referred to in this case quite well?

A: Yes; I have never seen it quite close. As a matter of fact, it is right underneath the car.

Q: You never had one loose before?

A: I have only had one previous Morris Minor car.

Q: You have never had in any car that union joint loose?

A: Yes.

Q: Leaking petrol?

A: Yes, before now.

Q: Did it come onto the floor of the car?

A: No, the Morris Minor is the only car that has had the union in that position.

Q: You know perfectly well, do you not, that if you get a loose joint there you can get quite a steady flow of petrol on to the floor of the car?

A: If you had a very loose joint.

Why does Rouse admit he knows enough to set a fire like the one he is accused of setting? Is it candour (trying to stay as close to the truth as possible), fear of what the advocate might know, a reluctance to admit ignorance, or a desire to show that leaking union joints are a common phenomena? Whatever his reason, as soon as Rouse admits that he has experienced a leaking union

joint before, Birkett quickly follows with a leading question which
secures the admission he requires.

Rouse has now demonstrated knowledge of the means of
carrying out the alleged crime, a key part of establishing
opportunity. When reading this next passage remember the point
made about a witness who lies; all their answers point one way.

Q: Do you doubt yourself that the flame came from any other
source than that joint?

A: That is a rather technical question.

Finnemore: With all respect, is that a question for this
                  witness?

Judge: The witness is entitled to refuse to answer it if
                  he likes.

Birkett continues: Leave it, Rouse. I wanted to put it quite plainly,
                  because I am going to suggest that one of the
                  places you lit that car was at that source.

A: I did not light the car. When you say 'Lit the car' is it not
evident to anybody that if I had lit the car, anybody, especially
as you admit I have some knowledge of cars, to light petrol or
petrol vapour you get a flash of some considerable degree,
especially if you loosen a joint. You would have to wait a
minute or so before you strike a light, and in that case you
would get a flash, and in that case, being near it, striking the
match, would be singed; and that is the first thing the police
officers looked at, and I offered my hands in the first place.

Q: You make the answer that you understand the problem of
lighting petrol quite well?

A: I have lit petrol, because I have a blow lamp at home.

Birkett, in his closing speech, says of Rouse:

'You might very well think an innocent man might say 'I really
don't know' but he has got it (an explanation for everything).
He is resourceful, he cannot resist the temptation to explain.'

6.8   Ending a cross-examination

The ending of a cross-examination will be remembered by those trying the issue of fact. Because of this it may be important in assessing the credibility of a witness. For this reason a cross-examination should not 'fizzle out'. Even if the witness' evidence has not been destroyed the advocate can still end on a high note. The use of a line of insinuating questions is a good option for closing the cross-examination of an important witness for the other side. This is the end of Birkett's cross-examination of Rouse:

Q: I am suggesting to you that yours was the hand that fired that car.

A: It was not.

Q: And that at the time you fired that car your companion, picked up upon the road, was unconscious?

A: No.

Q: And that he was unconscious by your hand?

A: No.

Q: And that he had been thrown into that unconscious position, face forwards, into the car which you were to light?

A: Most decidedly not. I should not throw a man. If I did a thing like that, I should not throw him face forwards. I should think where I put him, I imagine.

Birkett's final question was:

Q: And you lied for two days?

A: The lies that you put to me I will admit; yes.

6.9   Cross-examining expert witnesses

An advocate cross-examining an expert may appear to be at a disadvantage because she is generally asking questions in the expert's domain, not her own. However, assuming that the necessary preparation has been done there are several approaches which can be effective in cross-examining an expert witness:

- narrowing the basis of the expert's opinion to assumptions of questionable validity, taking his position to an' illogical extreme

- identifying the basis of particular assertions and examining the assumptions underlying each element

- demonstrating that the expert's opinion was formed without access to basic information or was based on inaccurate information

- showing errors in calculations

- ridiculing the status, experience or qualifications of the expert

Hypothetical questions can be used for the first two of these options. For example, if an expert says that concrete was inadequate for use in a coach park, hypothetical questions might show that it would be suitable for a car park. This establishes that it is the use to which the concrete is put rather than the concrete itself which is the basis of the expert's opinion that the 'concrete is inadequate'.

The advocate has the choice of several styles of cross-examination for experts; destructive, neutralising and utilising.

- **Destructive** cross-examination attacks the witness on the grounds of their credentials, their experience or their expertise

- **Neutralising** cross-examination leaves credibility intact but marginalises the impact of the testimony

- **Utilising** cross-examination uses the other side's witness to boost the credibility of your own expert

Baldwin classifies these different styles of cross-examination in terms of the degree of risks carried by different strategies:

Low risk strategies include:

- corroborating cross-examination: the expert is asked to agree with points in your favour

- discrediting cross-examination: exploiting strong material suggesting lack of foundation for expert opinion or improbabilities in opinion

Medium risk strategies include:

- raising a question over qualifications: a mechanical engineer may have technical qualification but do these relate to the specific problem?

- exploiting inconsistent testimony: previous answers inconsistent with known facts, ordinary human experience, with lay witness testimony. Establishing that facts were not revealed to the expert

High risk strategies include:

- probing with no particular aim

- personal attack on credentials

- claiming lack of foundation for opinion from weak material, arguing on expert's ground

- emphasising only 'your opinion'

Baldwin (1984)

Let's look at a fairly low risk strategy for cross-examination of a medical expert. Assume that the defendant's medical expert in a personal injury case says in examination-in-chief:

'In my opinion Mary Smith suffered no permanent injury as the result of the accident on May 5th.'

His advocate may continue and ask for the basis of the opinion. He may not. He may know that his expert will stand up well to cross-examination on this point. Instead, he wants you to ask for the basis for the opinion. Your cross-examination may struggle because you are being asked to embark on a high risk strategy. You may sit down with the witness ahead. An alternative is to continue as follows:

Q: Doctor; how many times did you examine Mary Smith?

A: One time.

Q: Doctor, would it surprise you if I were to tell you that Dr Jones examined Mary Smith 23 times over the course of two and a half years?

A: No.

Q: Is Dr Jones a respected member of the medical profession?

A: Yes he is.

Q: Thank you very much Doctor. That's all I have.

Greenwald (1983)

(See also McElhaney (1977))

Finnemore called forensic experts on behalf of Rouse, among them Herbert Bamber and Arthur Isaacs. Both argued that the fire could have started accidentally. Birkett cross-examined the first, Herbert Bamber. What kind of cross-examination is this; destructive, neutralising or utilising? What degree of risk do you think it carries?

Q: Have you had much experience of fires with regard to motor cars?

A: There are quite a number of cases where I have been called in to try and find out the reason of certain car fires, but that is all.

Q: Your principal avocation is collisions between motor cars, is it not?

A: Not all together - crane accidents, and all sorts of engineering matters.

Q: Again, in this particular region when you are called to give evidence, it is usually upon a collision and the result of a collision between two cars?

A: Yes, very frequently.

Q: As to fires in cars you have not had much experience in that department?

A: Not as much as fire assessors, naturally. I myself would of course pay the greatest respect to the opinions of men of experience like Colonel Buckle (the prosecution expert).

Arthur Isaacs, engineer and fire assessor, volunteered evidence for the defence having seen reports of the proceedings. The main point he wished to make was that the finding that the nut on the union joint was a whole turn loose was a phenomenon invariably observed after intense fires. He explained that metal distorted as it cooled to produce this effect. This was a witness with considerable experience of car fires who also offered a plausible explanation of how the fire could have started.

> 'He (the dead man) puts his left knee on the seat of the car and rests his hand on the steering wheel to pick up the can from the driver's seat. Lifting the can up it is possible that he overbalanced and fell forward on his face, with the result that the petrol - I am assuming the top was fairly loose - was spilled over the place - a good deal of it - and from what he was smoking, a cigar or cigarette, the fire would take place. The cigar would ignite the vapour which would be made the moment the vapour mixed with the air.'

The next excerpt is taken from the cross-examination of Issacs. Remember in reading it whenever possible the start of a cross-examination should make an impact. The audience is most alert at that point; the witness may be apprehensive; it is an opportunity for the advocate to secure a psychological advantage and to fix an image of the witness in the mind of the jury. What kind of cross-examination is this next example; destructive, neutralising or utilising? What degree of risk do you think it carried?

Q: What is the co-efficient of expansion of brass?

A: I am afraid I cannot answer that question off-hand.

Q: If you do not know say so. What do I mean by the term?

A: You want to know what is the expansion of metal under heat?

Q: I asked you what is the co-efficient of the expansion of brass. Do you know what that means?

A: Put that way I probably do not.

Q: You are an engineer?

A: I dare say I am. I am not a doctor, nor a crime investigator, nor an amateur detective. I am an engineer.

And later

Q: If a nut is loosened, is it loosened because it is expanded by heat and so be enabled to be loosened?

A: That is right.

Q: Therefore, do you not think it is important in telling a jury in so important a case that conclusion, that you should know, within limits, how much brass expands when subjected to heat?

A: I do.

Q: But you do not know?

A: Yes, I tell them I do not know.

In his speech to the ABA Sir Norman Birkett recalled that particular cross-examination

> 'Any case of notoriety always brings out people from all parts of the land volunteering to give evidence ... And there was I rising to cross-examine him, and whether it was inspiration or what it was I do not know, but my first question to the man was certainly not in the brief. I said 'tell me sir, what is the coefficient of expansion of brass?' And he didn't know. I am not sure I did, but he couldn't ask me questions and I could ask him, and he didn't know. And from that moment of course, it was easy.'

6.10 Cross-examining police officers

There are special difficulties in cross-examining police officers. Gone are the days when their evidence is beyond suspicion and rules for cross-examining police witnesses on their own credibility are well established (see Archbold (1993) especially paras 8-127 to 128). However, unjustified attacks on the honesty of police officers will antagonise the court.

> 'There is a growing tendency among some young advocates to give vent to privately held views, often political in nature, by questioning police officers in an openly insulting tone. An emotionally motivated advocate always damages his own case.'
>
> Bartle (1983)

While recent experience shows that some police officers do lie remember that error is more common than dishonesty. Friendly cross-examination is more likely to elicit acceptance of the possibility of error. Your approach can be subtle; suspend judgement until you hear what the officer has to say. If, for example, the evidence of several officers bears remarkable similarities you might ask the following questions:

- have you discussed the case with colleagues?
- did you do that before or after making up your notes?
- how soon were the notes made up?
- what was the nature of the discussion?
- who was there?
- was my client's role in the incident discussed?

What progress you make will depend on the answers you get. You might find that different officers give different responses to the questions. That may, in itself, give you the material you need for your closing speech.

Obviously, it is vitally important to be aware of the Codes of Practice made under the Police and Criminal Evidence Act (1984) since under s 78(1) the prosecution may be denied the opportunity to present evidence which in the circumstances, 'including the circumstances in which the evidence was obtained', there would be an 'adverse effect on the fairness of the proceedings'. Codes of Practice C (governing detention and questioning of suspects) and Code E (governing the tape recording of statements) are particularly relevant to the admissibility of confessions.

6.11 Re-examination

The right to re-examine your witness after cross-examination arises only in relation to points covered in cross-examination. Whether or not to re-examine is not an easy decision. You may draw attention to points on which you think the cross-examiner scored. You are not allowed to lead the witness and they may be mystified about what it is you are hoping they will say. Your mutual confusion may make the situation worse. Sometimes you may wish a witness to expand an answer which the cross-examiner cut off. If a witness has given evidence in cross-examination which you think was a slip of the tongue you may have to bite the bullet, particularly if the point was important.

The following is Finnemore's re-examination of Arthur Isaacs in which he tries to undo the damaging insinuation against Isaacs' competence.

Q: Do you know, from a metallurgical point of view, why a nut which is subject to intense heat, afterwards, when it cools, is in fact loose? Do you know of the metallurgical explanation or not?

A: No, I cannot say that I do.

Q: But you say, from your experience, that it happens?

A: Yes in every case that I have had.

Q: You do not profess to be a metallurgist?

A: No, not at all.

Finnemore's questions try to re-establish Isaacs' credibility as an expert. They suggest that Isaacs' inability to answer Birkett's 'coefficient of expansion' question is because it relates to knowledge that is not part of his own discipline. Note the naming of the discipline in question; 'metallurgy'. Thus, the thrust of Finnemore's re-examination is that Isaacs is a competent engineer, not an incompetent metallurgist.

6.12   Summary

- always cross-examine with a purpose in mind and only enough to fulfil that purpose

- use probing questions to force the witness to commit to a position

- be civil but ensure you control the witness

- listen carefully to responses

- use a 'hostile' approach with caution

- try to end a cross-examination powerfully

- select from destructive, neutralising and utilising strategies when cross-examining experts

6.13 End of chapter references and additional reading

Archbold M I   *Archbold Pleadings, Evidence*
(1993)   *and Practice in Criminal cases*
                      Vol 1 Ch 8
                      Sweet & Maxwell

Baldwin S   *Jury Argument*
(1984)   Trial Vol 20 No 4

Du Çann R   *The Art of the Advocate*
(1980)   Ch 6
                      Penguin

Greenwald   *Let Me Ask You This.....Some*
(1983)   *Thoughts on Cross-Examination*
                      Trial Vol 19 No 6

Hain P   *Mistaken Identity: The Wrong face*
(1976)   *of the Law*
                      Quartet Books

McElhaney J W   *Cross-Examining Expert*
(1977)   *Witnesses*
                      Litigation Vol 3 No 4

Munkman J   *The Technique of Advocacy*
(1991)   Ch 5
                      Butterworth

Murphy P   *A Practical Approach to Evidence*
(1992)   Ch 14
                      Blackstone Press

Stone M   *Cross-Examination in Criminal*
(1988)   *Trials*
                      Butterworth

Younger I   *A Letter in which Cicero Lays*
(1977)   *Down the Ten Commandments*
                             of Cross-Examination
                             Litigation Vol 3 No 2

CHAPTER

7 Summarising and Concluding

'Sincerity is the cornerstone of an effective jury address. Do not be carried away by ostentation and flamboyance. Do not let the jurors feel that you are trying to be superior to them. Do not talk at them - reason with them.'

Levy (1981)

7.1 The importance of summary

Even in the simplest case, where there have been only ten minutes of argument, there are merits in a short review of the issues prior to a submission. Often a Master will say to the solicitors 'do you have anything more you wish to say?' and both will say 'Master, no'. This is a chance to deliver the speech that you will have prepared on the assumption that everything would go well. You could respond by saying:

'I am grateful Master. For me to succeed with this application I must establish three things; first ...'

Be concise but show you know exactly what you are doing. Show you expect to win. Make it difficult to turn you down. If the Master had made up his mind you might just change it. In concluding any presentation to a court it is important to review what has gone before accurately and fairly. Some lawyers think that the result has already been determined by the time any concluding remarks are made. However, there are others who believe firmly in the power of summaries to convince and there are, no doubt, some cases where the issues are so finely balanced that the ending determines the outcome.

7.2 Closing speeches to juries

A closing speech to a jury should be prepared before trial; as with any other closing submission it should be based on what you expect to have proved. Obviously you will make adjustments according to the evidence which has been presented. You will, for example, be able to comment on the evidence given by particular witnesses. The total effect of damage done by cross examination may not be obvious to the jury. Here is your opportunity to weave the materials and evidence into coherent argument. The style should be conversational, streamlined and functional. Your oratory should not be ornate; your aim should be to convince the jury that your client has a good case, not that you are a brilliant advocate.

> 'Argument must be approached from a practical standpoint in keeping with reality as against the old notion that oratory is golden and irrefutably persuasive.'
>
> Levy (1981)

In setting out to persuade the ideal format would be one to one discussion, the atmosphere would be solemn and you would be earnest. While you need some emotion, keep this well under control. James McElhaney has written about an incident in an American case in where the defendant was charged with illegal gun running. The defence advocate was using the device of the rhetorical question to try to 'weave a spell' over the jury:

> 'The defendant's final argument was that the prosecution simply had a 'paper case'. The defence lawyer was trying to weave a spell. He would pick up document after document holding each aloft, while shouting the rhetorical question 'what does this prove?' Finally, to nail it down, he picked up a whole handful and shouted 'what do they all prove?' Juror number 5 answered the defence lawyer's question out loud. 'Illegal dealing in guns?'
>
> McElhaney (1985)

Would you say that this advocate's mistake was:

(a) risky use of the rhetorical question or

(b) trying to manipulate the jury?

Which would you say is the worse mistake?

If you have laid your groundwork you will have identified and played to your emotional strengths throughout the trial; now is the time for the logical argument which justifies the jury's emotional predisposition towards your case. Talk to members of the jury by maintaining eye contact with each. You can often assume that the jury will be split and that some will convince the others. If you can identify potential leaders you may choose to look at them a little more frequently precisely because you hope that they will be more persuasive. Do not let the jurors think that you feel superior to them. Acknowledge, if you like, the difficulty of their task.

One QC writes of a lawyer who, in his closing address warned the jury 'not to play God'. The author was later told by a juror that many members of the jury were deeply offended by the remark.

Martin (1967)

Organise your material carefully. Every good jury address since the time of Cicero has had three parts: an introduction; the argument and, finally, peroration (the last part of a lengthy speech).

7.3   Closing speeches to juries for the defence

7.3.1   Introduction

The introduction may be used to underline the grave responsibilities they have assumed and the dangers of erroneous conviction.

You can reinforce this with an outline of the basic principles which they are bound to apply, such as the presumption of innocence. Remember that research in the United States found that successful defence lawyers often used vague language and included discussion of vague concepts in their speeches (see also para 1.7 in Chapter One). 'Reasonable doubt' is a classic example of a suitably vague concept. In the first paragraph of his closing speech in the Rouse case Finnemore moved swiftly to the burden of proof:

> '... You will perform this high task of citizenship committed to you on the evidence which has been called in the case during this week. I refer straight away to the main guiding and dominating issues in the trial, and, I suggest to you, they show that the case for the prosecution has completely broken down, falling utterly short of that amount of legal proof which is needed. Rouse is entitled to a verdict of acquittal ...'

You may wish to emphasise the important role that these basic principles play in guaranteeing the civil liberties of the jurors as well as those of your client. You may, at this stage, remind the jury of the indictment and explain what the prosecution needs to prove in relation to each part.

You may choose to attempt to convey confidence by telling the jury what they should do. Some writers on advocacy warn against this. It is human nature when someone says 'You cannot convict this man!' to think 'Oh yes we can'. However, if you weave the judge's likely instructions to the jury into your speech their confidence in you may increase when the judge repeats those points. Hopefully the instruction will also trigger recollection of what you told them on that point.

You may choose not to dwell on the burden of proof but instead to be positive in advancing your own theory of the case. Frank Cicero argues that 'the prosecution have not proved their case' is not a psychologically appealing argument. What does 'reasonable doubt' mean to a jury? What does it mean to a lawyer for that matter?

Cicero (1982)

Your introduction should also prepare the jury for your argument. Wherever possible refer to the client by name; do not refer to him as 'the accused' or 'the defendant'. By personalising your client it is probably easier to make points about his rights and the jury's duties to a fellow citizen. There may be particular circumstances which need to be dealt with. Not every defendant is a wholly sympathetic person. The jury may need reminding that they are trying the accused for the offence charged and on the evidence presented, not on press speculation, notoriety or personal appearance. You should, however, have confidence that the jury will do its duty. If you are able to present your client as someone of 'good character', make the most of this. A jury will readily accept that someone who has habitually maintained a good record in his dealings will not suddenly change character, either by committing an offence or by lying on oath.

7.3.2   The argument

You will review the evidence for both sides. In your review you should not go into the detail of what every witness said; instead, summarise the main point of their evidence. Organise it in a way which makes it accessible. Evidence presented in a haphazard way is confusing and does not help you to make a persuasive argument. If your review is difficult to follow the jury may become bored and stop listening.

A typical order for the argument stage is:

- destruction of case for prosecution and

- deploying evidence for defence

One way to begin your review is to go through the prosecution's case, highlighting those elements where the evidence falls short of the required standard of proof. Appeal to the jury's experience and common sense. List the improbabilities of the prosecution case; things which the jury would expect to be satisfied of if the client was guilty. Often this will involve subjecting the evidence to quite minute analysis and advancing a theory of the case which best explains that evidence. Here, for example, is a small part of Lewis Hawser's analysis in the Hain case:

'The glasses are a crucial point in this case, and for this reason: (boys 1 and 2) have said that they are quite certain that the thief in Werter Road was wearing glasses. I am putting it to you that they are quite wrong in this. I have not suggested that they lied about it, but because they thought that the man in the Volkswagen might be the same man, and he was wearing glasses, they thought back and assumed that the first man had been wearing glasses ...'

Notice how Hawser avoids calling the boys liars. This illustrates a point well made by Keith Evans. Courts will invariably find explanations of contradictions more acceptable where an innocent explanation of the contradictions is plausible. This is what Evans calls 'showing them the way home' - allowing the court to reach 'the right decision' without having to decide that the other side must be lying.

Evans (1992)

Improbabilities can be posed as questions both for the jury to consider and for the prosecution to answer. This is particularly effective when you know there is no answer. However, even when there is a credible response it forces the prosecution onto your ground and this may involve some adjustment of the prosecution closing speech.

If the offence was robbery, for example:

- was any money found?
- was there evidence that the client had been spending large sums of money?
- did the client need money for some purpose?

It may also be necessary to explain any adverse facts which may trouble the jury. Anticipate any closing by the other advocate and steal their thunder by confronting their best points. If there is accomplice evidence against your client, for example, you might find that this evidence is convincing. How can you best explain that evidence? The accomplice was there; the only lie he needs to remember is the one which implicates the accused. It is easier to be convincing when telling only one lie. What is his motive for lying? The motive might be grievance, the hope of a light sentence for himself or protection of a friend. You should have a good idea of which explanation the jury will find most plausible after cross-examining the accomplice.

Having cast doubt on the prosecution case, outline the defence theory of the case. Be careful not to refer to 'the theory of the case' because, to a juror, this sounds like 'lawyer speak' for a plausible story. You are not telling a plausible story; you are telling the jury what really happened.

If the accused was not called to give evidence it is probably best not to mention this unless you are able to say that he gave a full account in a statement and does not wish to add to this.

Where the accused does testify, this fact should be referred to as a sign of his innocence. If the accused was a good witness you can suggest that 'only an innocent man could withstand such an excellent cross-examination'. If, however, the accused was a poor witness this can be explained by the strain which he was undoubtedly under. Look at this short extract from Finnemore's closing speech in the Rouse case. What do you think is the sub-text of each sentence?:

> 'He has told his own story, though he was not bound to give evidence, and he has been subjected for three hours to a minute, searching and vigorous cross-examination. Nothing new came out, and the story that he told remained as it started, and was, in substance, the same story that he told in his statement at Hammersmith. You might think that he was voluble and excitable; you know from Dr Telling that is his temperament. He is suffering from a head wound he received in the war and was facing the most trying ordeal any man could be called on to face. You must ask yourselves, is his story true? Panic is a well-known thing, and you all have sufficient knowledge of human nature to know that it is not unlikely for some people, in the face of sudden emergency and terror, to lose their nerve and, instead of helping, to become possessed with the idea of getting away as quickly as possible ...'

In most cases the accused will be spared having any criminal record put before the court unless and until a finding of guilt has been made. However, there may be instances where the defence uses a criminal past as part of its case. One such example is the Mancini trial in which Birkett appeared for the defence. Birkett used Mancini's criminal record to explain the defendant's behaviour on discovering his girlfriend's battered body in their flat. Mancini had destroyed evidence, carried the victim's body around in a trunk and tried to arrange an alibi before his arrest. Birkett's explanation for this conduct was that Mancini believed that the police would think that he involved in his girlfriend's murder because of his criminal record.

You may have the opportunity to bolster evidence which was attacked by the prosecution. Alibi evidence, for example, will often be provided by the family or friends of the accused and is liable to be viewed with suspicion for that reason. This can be explained to the jury in terms which they can readily understand. For example:

'If any of you gentlemen were accused of having committed a crime at 3 o'clock in the morning, is there anyone who could prove where you were at that time other than your wife?'

Martin (1967)

Sometimes you may have the luxury of time to prepare your closing argument in advance. Advance preparation does not mean that you should write out exactly what you would like to say. You can use your time to think carefully about the organisation of your material. You might, for example, use a topical approach, looking at both defence and prosecution evidence in relation to each incident. This was the approach adopted by Finnemore in the Rouse case. Here is a topical map of his argument which I have constructed based on his speech:

Mind map of closing speech in the Rouse trial

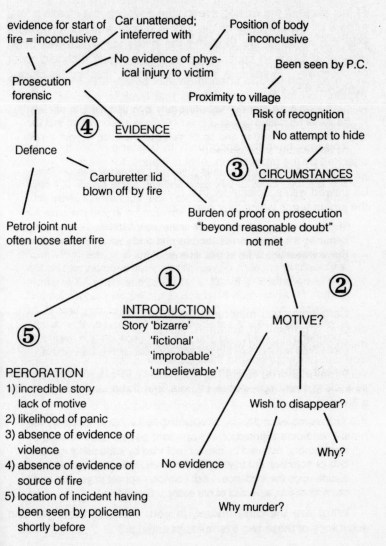

7.3.3   Peroration

At this stage of the closing speech the advocate may make a final appeal to the emotions of the jury in a way which is consistent with the mood of the trial and the evidence which has been presented. Such an appeal must be finely judged. It should never be overstated. Finnemore, in the Rouse trial, finished his closing speech in this way:

> '... But do not forget that your first duty is to that man, to see that he is not convicted unless and until you are all convinced that the evidence is so strong and so certain that it leaves in your minds no reasonable doubt whatever.
>
> Let me conclude by reminding you of your great responsibility. You are the judges of this case and you alone decide it. I have put the case for the prisoner before you, but I cannot share your responsibility. My learned friend will sum up to you the case for the prosecution, but he cannot share your burden. Not even my lord, who will direct you on the law and guide you, can share it on the evidence. It is yours alone. And it is the individual responsibility of each of you. When your foreman returns the verdict he returns it for all of you, but it is really 12 separate verdicts for which each must account to his own judgement and conscience. No man can be convicted in this country until all 12 jurymen say, 'we are satisfied beyond all reasonable doubt'. Consider your verdict as you will look back on it in weeks to come. You are the final judges and your decision is irrevocable.'

Birkett's closing speech in the Mancini trial is widely regarded as a classic example of the art. His final three sentences provide a flavour:

> 'And members of the jury, in returning that verdict (not guilty) you will vindicate a principle of law - that people are not tried by newspapers, not tried by rumour, not tried by statements made of love or notoriety, but tried by British juries, called to do justice and decide upon the evidence. I ask you for, I appeal to you for, and I claim from you, a verdict of not guilty ... Stand firm.'

What are the differences, in your view, in the style and substance of these two examples of endings?

7.4   Closing speeches to juries for the prosecution

The prosecution case to a jury will follow a very similar sequence to that outlined above. You will recall that research has shown that the prosecution benefits from a direct approach and forceful language (see also para 2.7 in Chapter Two); this display of certainty is no doubt calculated to sweep away any doubt which the jury may have about the case. Birkett, in his closing speech in the Rouse trial, paid compliments to Finnemore for his handling of the defence and continued:

'... this evidence conclusively, decisively, completely, beyond any human doubt, indicates that the accused in the early morning of the 6th November in that deserted lane, committed a deliberate, a calculated and a horrible murder. My learned friend says 'Let the prosecution tell you the motive'. The motive, if motive there be, is locked in the accused's own heart, and there is no power under heaven which enables me to unlock it. My learned friend has asked me to do an impossible thing - to satisfy you as to motive. My learned friend says 'Let the Crown satisfy you beyond all reasonable doubt where the light was put in the car'. If this was murder there is only one man who knows with surety. My learned friend says 'Don't convict this man until the Crown does the impossible ...'

Analyse the extract above. What is it which makes it persuasive? What is the significance of the content of the paragraph in relation to its location in the speech as a whole?

Now ask the same questions about the following passage of argument:

'My learned friend put the accused before you as a truthful man, despite the record of lies, invented say the defence, because of panic. But you may think that, in the accused, you have a man of resource, and you may think that the decisive thing in this case is the evidence that he gave. And you may test it by one or two of the most important matters. After two days this truthful man made his statement to the police and said 'I saw the man inside the car and tried to open the door'. Did he make a mistake about a thing like that? Then in the witness box he said 'I could not get near it, I never saw the man, and the doors were both shut' Is that the truth? ... As to the time you may make a mistake, as to the precise place you may make a mistake, and as to the distance from a village you may make a pardonable mistake; but the dead man - the companion of the night - he did not make a mistake ...'

Below there follows an example of Birkett's use of a rhetorical question. What, to your mind, is the significance of this rhetorical question, posed by Birkett in relation to Rouse's evidence, in terms of (a) presentation, and (b) substance?

'One factor in this very remarkable case which you may consider to be particularly remarkable is this: Do you think, upon reflection, that it is very remarkable that the accused had got a complete explanation for the theory of an accident - namely petrol and match?'

Was this a 'safe' question in the circumstances? If so, what makes it 'safe'?

The jury in the Rouse trial took only one hour and fifteen minutes to find him guilty of murder. He was sentenced to death. His appeal to the Court of Appeal was dismissed. On 11th March 1931, the day after Rouse's execution a letter from Rouse was published in the Daily Sketch. In it Rouse admitted the murder. It is curious how the detail confirms many of the tentative inferences the prosecution had drawn. Rouse had intended to 'disappear'. The dead man was a vagrant whom he had offered a lift. He had believed that fire would prevent identification and disguise the forensic evidence. He also thought a fire would be less noticeable on Guy Fawkes night, the night of the murder. He had strangled the man, loosened the petrol union joint and taken the top off the carburettor. He then doused the man with petrol and made a trail of petrol to the car which he lit with a match. He had intended to walk to Northampton and catch a train to Scotland. When he saw the men on Hardingstone Lane he knew his plan had miscarried. He hesitated at the top of the lane before deciding to go back to London.

7.5   Summary

- prepare your closing speech before the hearing
- be brief but persuasive
- do not lecture
- divide your speech into introduction, argument and peroration
- explain how the adverse evidence should be interpreted
- finally, deal with the other side's case and give an overview of your own

7.6   End of chapter references and additional reading

Cicero F   *Non Defensive Final Argument*
(1982)   *for the Defence*
                            Litigation Vol 8 No 3

Du Cann R   *The Art of the Advocate*
(1980)   Chs 10-11
                            Penguin Books

Evans K   *Advocacy at the Bar:*
(1992)   *A Beginner's Guide*
                            Blackstone Press

Levy E J   *The Closing Address*
(1981)   *by Defence Counsel*
                            Criminal Law Quarterly Vol 24

Martin G A   *Closing Arguments to the Jury*
(1967)   *for the Defence in Criminal Cases*
                            Criminal Law Quarterly

McElhaney J   *Illegal Dealing in Guns*
(1985)   *Breaking the spell*
                            Litigation Vol 12 No 1

CHAPTER

8

Advocacy in Practice 1

Criminal proceedings

Example One: Making an application for bail

8.1 Context

Under the Bail Act (1976) there is a presumption in favour of bail and reasons should be given for refusal. On an application for bail, either the prosecution or the court can raise objections; these usually emanate from the police. The defence advocate will usually have an opportunity to cross-examine the police officer on the reasons for the objection. The reasons typically relate to the seriousness of the charge, the possibility that the defendant will not appear at the hearing or some other reason such as the continuation of enquiries or possible interference with witnesses. The defence advocate will then make an application which addresses any objection. In considering the application the magistrates should bear in mind not only the seriousness of the offence, and the safety of the public, but also the evidence against the accused.

Previous convictions should not be read out in court but adduced in writing. Where the accused has a prima facie right to bail, magistrates must give written reasons for refusal. If bail is refused by magistrates, you should discuss with the client the prospects of renewing application at a later date or appeal to the Crown Court (see Bail Act (1976) s 5(6A)). If bail is granted subject to sureties entering undertakings these undertakings can be entered into before the magistrate. If sureties are not present in court, the undertakings can be given later to the magistrates or their clerk, a police officer who is at least an inspector or the governor of a prison or remand centre (see also para 9A Sched 1 Bail Act (1976)).

8.2   Preparing for a bail application

Since, for practical purposes, the first application for bail probably
has the best chance of success, choose your time well and
counsel your client accordingly. In preparing to make an
application there a number of sensible steps which should be
taken to give your client the best opportunity of being granted bail.
In addition to sureties you will wish to investigate the possibility of
the client agreeing to the following:

- residence at a particular address (eg with relative or at a bail
  hostel)

- giving an undertaking to keep away from a particular locality or
  reporting to a local police station

- curfew

- surrender of passport

From discussion with the parties involved, you should be sure
that you can answer the following questions.

Having talked with your client:

- what are the client's previous convictions (if any)?

- has he ever committed an offence while on bail?

- does he have a surety?

- is this an offence for which he is likely to be granted bail?

- is he likely to get a prison sentence (against which time spent
  on remand will be counted)?

- what are the possible prosecution objections and what
  conditions to bail might the prosecution set?

- does the client understand the implications of possible
  conditions and is he prepared to accept them?

Having talked with the proposed surety:

- does the surety understand the implications of standing as
  surety?

- how much can he raise and from what source?

  (Note: courts prefer a surety to have readily accessible money; not for example, the equity in a home.)

- what is his relationship to the accused?
- does he understand the consequences of the accused absconding?
- what capital/ savings does he have?
- what other liabilities does he have?
- how soon could the money be made available?

  Having talked with the probation officer (if any):

- does he anticipate any problems or objections and how can these be met?
- has he any practical suggestions for changing client's circumstances in order to meet possible conditions?
- can he offer any practical assistance in improving client's prospects?
- you might also ask the officer in the case whether the client has ever absconded or committed offences while on bail

  At this point you should evaluate the case and ask yourself:

- how realistic are the prospects on this charge, with these facts, with these antecedents and with the proposed sureties?

  Next you should discuss the case with the prosecutor:

- ask for details of evidence against client
- check antecedents against client's account
- ask for details of possible objections to bail
- suggest bail conditions which may address these concerns (if appropriate)

Make a final analysis of arguments for and against granting bail:

- was the alleged offence likely to be a 'one off'?

- have the client's circumstances changed and how?

- how might any change in circumstances make the client a 'good risk'?

- how strong is the case against your client?

    Be realistic

- deal with circumstances of the offence underlining any positive points in your client's favour, particularly the strong chances of acquittal or the unlikelihood of a custodial sentence

- outline any circumstances which would support the notion that your client will appear at subsequent hearings, for example family, employment or community ties

- propose conditions which will address legitimate concerns about this client's entitlement to bail

- deal with consequences of refusal for employment, family etc

8.3   Structure

The structure and content of a bail application depends to a large extent on the practice of the particular court and the objections which are raised to bail.

Having heard the objections you will then need to respond to them in a logical order or, if there is one main objection, break it down into its component parts and deal with each in turn.

If you have been forewarned of objections you will have been able to plan a structure for your response. Whether or not this has been possible you may wish to begin by challenging the validity of the objection(s).

In some cases however you may feel that such a challenge is unlikely to have any real chance of success. In such cases you should concentrate on measures which can meet the objection.

Finally, you will draw attention to the defendant's personal circumstances and the personal, domestic and employment consequences of a decision to deny the defendant his liberty.

At the end of your speech you will introduce any sureties.

8.4   Style

In bail applications it is important to remember that the court may have legitimate concerns about granting bail to your client. This is one of those occasions where subtlety usually prevails over a strong presentation. The court may need to be reassured that the decision to grant bail will not be one they might regret. Napley advises that:

> 'When applying for bail, both in cross-examination and argument, remember that your best chance of success lies in displaying such moderation and responsibility that the objections are made to look more unreasonable and unjust.'

> Napley (1991)

Example two: Making a plea in mitigation

Bartle describes the plea in mitigation as 'probably the most important function of the advocate at the magisterial level of the judicial structure'. A plea in mitigation is made after conviction on a 'not guilty' plea or after a plea of guilty. Even if your client is pleading 'not guilty' it is wise to prepare the plea in mitigation in advance in case the defence is not successful.

8.5   Context

8.5.1   The Criminal Justice Act 1991

The Criminal Justice Act 1991 (or CJA) makes a number of changes to criminal procedure which will impact on the way in which pleas in mitigation are presented. The central proposal in the White Paper was that the Act should provide 'a coherent framework for the use of financial, community and custodial punishments'. In many respects the Act 'does little more than confirm existing conventions' (Thomas 1992). However you should note the following:

- the guiding principle for deciding sentence is proportionality of custodial sentences to the gravity of the offence

- pre-sentence reports (see on para 8.6) prepared by probation officers are now mandatory except in limited circumstances

- the court may not pass a custodial sentence unless the requirement of 'seriousness' is satisfied (see on para 8.5.2) or

    i)   the offence is a violent or sexual offence and a custodial sentence is necessary to protect the public

    ii)   the court may combine two offences provided that these two offences are 'associated'

    iii) where a community sentence is justifed the accused's consent to a community sentence has been refused where such consent is required

- the Act is generally intended to increase the use of non-custodial sentences by an increased use of community orders as alternatives to custody

- fines are now more closely related to 'ability to pay'

8.5.2   Who hears a plea in mitigation?

Magistrates hear cases which must be tried summarily. The most serious offences such as murder or robbery are heard by a judge and jury in the Crown Court. With offences which are triable either way, magistrates may proceed with committal proceedings if they feel their powers of sentencing are inappropriate for the particular offence. Alternatively they may hear the case and then commit it to the Crown Court for sentence. Broadly, magistrates convicting an adult offender of one offence which would have been triable on indictment may impose a sentence of 6 months imprisonment and/or a fine of up to £5,000 for any offence triable either way. I relation to two or more offences magistrates can impose an aggregate prison term of 12 months and/or fines of £5,000 for each offence. In considering the gravity of the offence it is these powers which they will have in mind (see also Emmins on Criminal Procedure (1992)).

8.5.3 Criteria for sentencing

A speech in mitigation should address the court on the gravity of the offence on the scale and it should bring to the attention of the court relevant mitigating circumstances. An advocate should prepare and deliver a plea in mitigation with a clear understanding of the legislative framework within which sentencing takes place. It is equally important to be aware of the manner in which judicial discretion may be exercised.

Section 1(2) of the Criminal Justice Act 1991 now allows the court to pass a custodial sentence only where the offence and one other offence associated with it are so serious that only a custodial sentence can be justified.

In all cases the most severe sentences must be reserved for the 'worst examples' of the particular offence. The Act makes new provisions in relation to some offences and, in particular, in relation to young offender (Wassik and Taylor (1991)). The scale of sentences for offences of that type is deduced from the decisions of the Court of Appeal in similar cases. Two cases are rarely identical in all their circumstances and there is always a discretionary element in sentencing decisions. The Court of Appeal's sentencing decisions do not create precedents as such; they offer guidelines.

According to Bartle (1983), magistrates are predisposed to impose a custodial sentence in cases involving:

i)   violence causing injury to person, particularly to police officers or other public servant carrying out their duties

ii) possession of offensive weapon, where the weapon is a knife

iii) supplying or offering to supply a class A drug

iv) theft by an employee from an employer

v)   prolonged course of fraud or dishonesty

vi) commission of a further similar offence during the currency of a suspended sentence

vii) certain crimes outraging public morals; living on the earnings of a prostitute, sale of pornography involving large profits

The Criminal Justice Act 1991 gives no guidance on the identification of specific offences which are serious enough to justify custodial sentences, although s 29(1) provides that, neither previous convictions or failure to respond to previous sentences shall be considered as reasons for a custodial sentence.

Following the Act the options for sentencing are:

- absolute or conditional discharge
- supervision order
- attendance centre order
- curfew order
- probation order
- community sentence order
- suspended sentence
- immediate custodial sentence

Offence seriousness is the sole criterion in deciding whether a 'community sentence' should be imposed. There is the additional criterion of public protection before sentencing an offender to custody for violent or sexual offences.

The sentence should be proportionate to the gravity of the offence. The sentence should not be increased beyond the appropriate point on the scale because the defendant has previous convictions or has pleaded not guilty. Previous convictions do not increase the 'seriousness of the offence'. However, before the CJA 1991 there was some evidence that judges occasionally increase the tariff sentence because of aggravating features. Under the CJA s 2(2)b the court can increase the length of the sentence for violent or sexual offences to such longer term (not exceeding the statutory maximum) as is necessary to protect the public. However, in general, the effect of previous convictions is more likely to be a decrease in the potency of any mitigation.

> 'The longer and more regular one's pattern of offending, the less mitigation one can expect. This progressive loss of mitigation continues to the point at which there is no mitigation to be lost.'
>
> Fitzmaurice and Pease (1988)

See also May LJ in *R* v *Fraser* (1982) 4 Cr App R (S) 254.

Having established the approximate sentence for the particular circumstances in which the offence was committed, mitigation potentially reduces the sentence below the standard sentence for those circumstances.

Emmins (1992) identifies three ways in which mitigation can affect sentence:

1 Reduction of punishment (shorter prison sentence, smaller fine or fewer hours of community service)

2 Different form of punishment (community sentences instead of prison)

3 Alternative to punishment (hospital orders)

Now, under the CJA s 3(3), information about the offender must not be taken into account in determining the length of a custodial sentence. However, the court must take into account information about the offender in deciding which community order or orders are 'most suitable for the offender' (s 6(2)(a) and s 7(2)).

8.6   Procedure

After a plea of guilty or finding of guilt there are three main stages before sentence is passed.

First, the prosecution will make a statement outlining the facts of the case. In the Crown Court this statement will be based on committal statements and will contain relevant details about the offence and the arrest and questioning of the accused by the police. The prosecution are under a duty to present the circumstances fairly. Nevertheless they will concentrate on any features which suggest that this is a 'bad' example of this type of offence. On some occasions it may be necessary to challenge facts alleged by the prosecution. If, after a not guilty plea, it appears that the defence is denying facts which are necessary elements of the charge the defendant will be invited to change his plea. If the offence is admitted but aggravating features are denied the judge should hear the evidence on the point or hear submissions from advocates in order to resolve the conflict. If the judge does base a decision on submissions and there is conflict in the different versions of the facts the defendant's version should be preferred wherever possible.

However, the judge should hear evidence where there is a dispute as to the facts which could affect sentence (*R* v *Newton* (1982) 77 Cr App R 13). If the judge does have a 'Newton hearing', and decides against the defence on the disputed facts, the accused may lose some of the mitigation he would have received for a guilty plea.

Emmins (1992)

Next, police evidence is taken regarding the defendant's character (previous conviction) and antecedents (background and circumstances). The police officer, having taken the oath, will read out the information or answer leading questions from the prosecution advocate. In the magistrates courts the procedure may be less formal with a Crown Prosecution representative merely handing in a list of previous convictions. It is the intention of the Act that antecedents should play a smaller part in determining sentence. However, it is not clear to what extent the principle of 'progressive loss of mitigation' has been retained by s 29(1) for repeat offenders (Wassik & Taylor (1991) p 27).

Under the *Practice Direction* (1966) 1 WLR 1184 the antecedents cover:

i) the accused's age and date of birth

ii) his education and previous and present employment

iii) the date of his arrest and details of whether he was detained or bailed since arrest

iv) a summary of his previous convictions and the date of his last discharge from prison and

v) his domestic circumstances

The defence may challenge any information given in the antecedents in which case the prosecution must establish the particular fact by producing evidence.

The next stage is for the court to call for pre-sentence reports. The Criminal Justice Act 1991 requires that the court obtain and consider a pre-sentence report before imposing a custodial sentence (s 3(1)) or making a probation order with additional requirements, a community service order or a combination order.

Pre-sentence reports are prepared by probation officers who are bound to offer a 'professional and impartial assessment of the offender's family, education and employment background and of social motivational and other circumstances related to the offending'. Under s 6(7) the report should include indications of 'suitable' community orders which might be made. However, the report will generally avoid recommending particular kinds of sentence.

Any character witnesses should be called to give evidence at this point.

Finally, the defence will present its plea in mitigation before sentence.

8.7   Lessons from research

Empirical research on sentencing can provide useful clues for preparing a successful plea in mitigation. In 'The Psychology of Judicial Sentencing', Fitzmaurice and Pease list a number of factors found in other research. Aggravating features typically relate to the way in which the crime was committed. Most of the mitigating factors relate to the personal characteristics and circumstances of the offender.

Aggravating factors:

Offender continued criminal activity after arrest

Offender showed erratic/ irrational behaviour in offence

Offender showed bizarre/ depraved behaviour in the offence

Police state arrest was difficult

Offender under influence of drugs at time

Offender under influence of alcohol at time

Offender a person of high status in community

Offender a person of no fixed abode

Instant offence repeats an earlier offence

Instant offence is of different type from earlier

Military record shows proven military crime

Offender does not express remorse eg found guilty but pleaded not guilty

Victim was particularly vulnerable

Injury to victim was unusually extensive

Damage to property was unusually extensive

Multiple injuries to victim

Victim is/ was friend

Victim is relation

Victim presses for heavy penalty

Evidence of planning of the crime

Much similar crime in district lately

Mitigating factors:

Offender is younger than usual for this crime

Offender offers/has made restitution

Offender assisted law officers in solving other crimes

Offender has exceptionally good employment record

Offender had been drinking at time

Offender of low intelligence

Offender's wife a serious problem/ family difficulties

Prior mental treatment

Physical handicap of offender

No arrests or convictions

No arrests or convictions except as juvenile

No previous crimes of same kind

No previous crimes but only arrests

Provocation seems likely

Victim is/ was a friend of offender

Victim asks for leniency

Political motive for crime

Others involved apparently leaders

Property recovered by police

Prison would cause exceptional hardship to offender's dependants

Fitzmaurice and Pease (1988)

Under the Criminal Justice Act 1991 s 3(3)(1) the court must take into account all known circumstances of an offence, both aggravating and mitigating but, when deciding whether or not the sentence should be custodial, the defendant's background is immaterial except in so far as it impacts on the circumstances of the offence as an aggravating factor. It seems likely, however, that future clarification will allow other mitigating points to be made before a custodial sentence is passed (Thomas (1992)).

For the present it is assumed that relevant considerations may include provocation, lack of premeditation and 'pressure akin to duress'. (Wassik & Taylor (1991) p 25). However, the Criminal Justice Act s 28(1) gives the court a discretion to consider mitigating factors which do not relate to the seriousness of the offence. It is therefore thought that the courts will continue to pay regard to the range of personal circumstances which are often included in mitigation speeches.

Emmins (1992)

Research carried out prior to the CJA 1991 analysed the factors mentioned in a sample of mitigation speeches. Circumstances relating to the offence were more likely to occur in speeches where there was a plea of guilty because the circumstances of the crime were not previously before the court. In order of frequency, these factors were:

(a) has job/ good job/ in work now

(b) good work record

(c) minor role/ part played by defendant

(d) sorry/ apologises/ contrite

(e) co-operated with police/ admitted offence

(f) settled relationship with family/ family responsibilities

(g) no previous conviction

(h) minor offence of its type

(i) kept out of trouble since last offence some time ago

(j) relatives present in court

(k) drink/ judgement marred by drink

(l) accepts must be punished/ go to prison. Offers compensation

(m) defendant was in financial difficulties. Has pleaded guilty

(n) unlikely to do it again (view of others). In custody now

There is a striking correlation between these factors and those traditionally appearing in pre-sentence reports (see above under para 8.4). Emmins regards four types of mitigation as 'especially common and cogent'; age, previous good character, a plea of guilty and co-operation with the police. More can be said about each of these and you are recommended to consult a specialist text (see, for example, Emmins on Criminal Procedure (1992). In general the value of tables like these is that they are indicative of what experience has revealed are successful mitigation points. This assumes that advocates do not persevere in making points which do not strike a chord; that may not be a justified assumption!

8.8   The audience

Research shows that magistrates' sentencing objectives do not vary significantly according to sex, age, education or religious or political affiliation. Further, whatever their sentencing objectives, their perceptions of the appropriateness or effectiveness of various sentencing options are reasonably consistent. A large majority think that prison has no 'treatment value'; instead imprisonment is the sentence chosen to mark the seriousness of the offence or to protect society, or as the last resort where the offender has failed to respond to other forms of disposal, for example probation or community service. The most significant factor influencing the choice of probation is the potential benefit to the offender. Community service represents a half-way house; 67% regard it as an effective treatment and 47% regard it as punishment. However, the major factor in choosing Community Service is the belief that the offender can benefit from it.

Henham (1990)

It is difficult to predict how the courts will react to the new provisions of the Criminal Justice Act which are intended to increase the punitive aspects of 'community sentences' and to reduce the relevance of a failure to respond to other forms of disposal (see s 29(1)). Mitigation points may change accordingly.

It is also true that different magistrates are responsive to different points which may be made in mitigation. Some courts even develop reputations for particular propensities; a folklore builds up whereby experienced advocates will say 'Such and such a court is tough on drink driving'. Magistrates receive approximately ten hours training in relation to the Act and this may well prove effective in standardising the approach in different courts. However, if you have experienced colleagues you should ask them about their experience of the court in question. Be conscious that their perception is personal to them; it is always worthwhile you sitting through a morning in any court where you may have to conduct advocacy.

8.9   Preparation

In preparing a plea in mitigation you should take the following steps:

- consider the charges and any statements
- interview the client to discover his version of events and his views on the case
- consider whether the offence/s have been committed
- consider the appropriate plea
- warn your client of any difficulties in a not guilty plea

- warn your client must not plead guilty if did not commit the offence

- what does the prosecution allege are the circumstances?

- if the plea is 'guilty', discuss whether there are any mitigating factors which should be brought to the attention of the court. You may run through a checklist of possible factors

- advise on the likely impact of mitigation with regard to the circumstances of the crime and previous offences

- consider whether any character witnesses are willing to give evidence, what they would be prepared to say and whether or not their evidence would be beneficial (are they of 'good character'?)

- if your client is remanded for a pre-sentence report advise on the effect of the report and impress on the client that this may be an opportunity to improve his position, for example by getting a job

You should analyse the aggravating features of the crime. Ask yourself the following questions:

- does the accused accept the facts asserted by the prosecution or might a 'Newton hearing' be necessary? (see para 8.6 above)

- what is the maximum sentence for an offence of this type and what sentencing guidelines are there, if any?

- what would be 'the worse type' of this kind of offence?

- what factors indicate that this is not an offence of the worse type?

- what aggravating features, if any, are there?

- what factors suggest a custodial sentence may be necessary? (do the public need to be protected from this defendant?)

- what mitigating features are there?

- what sentence is the court likely to pass on this defendant

8.10   Structure of a plea in mitigation

Many advocates structure the plea in mitigation around comment on the antecedents and the facts of case. They then move to consider the sentence which is appropriate in the particular case. It is a general principle that, whereas prosecuting counsel must never refer to sentence, the pleader in mitigation should try to suggest an appropriate course of action to the court.

Hyam (1990) argues against this 'compartmentalised approach'. He suggests that pleas in mitigation should flow entirely from sentencing guidelines, the facts being subordinate to the argument rather than its basis. This is, in essence, a topical organisation based on convincing the court that the circumstances of the crime suggest a sentence which is less severe than the norm for that offence. All facts or matters which do not ring true, cannot be corroborated or which are unrelated to sentencing guidelines should, Hyam suggests, be omitted, or at the very least treated with extreme caution. This approach is certainly consistent with the aims of the CJA 1991.

8.11   Content

The content of a speech in mitigation depends on the circumstances. You may wish to focus on the background reasons why the accused committed the offence or his prospects for the future. Employment, reconciliation, marriage or parenthood are all circumstances which offer reasons why offenders may wish to change the present direction of their lives.

If the crime was one of violence provocation, or where there was a pre-existing relationship with victim, you may wish to suggest that the defendant is not a risk to the public at large. Remorse, particularly coupled with guilty plea, is good mitigation. Signs of remorse are generally more potent than expressions of remorse. So, for example, where compensation has been offered the magistrates may be more inclined to defer sentence to allow the defendant to make restitution or to impose a fine coupled with suspended sentence. Where recompense has been made it is wise to have some evidence of this in court. Issues of race and gender have for some time been the subject of some controversy and suggestions that women and ethnic minorities are disproportionately punished are not uncommon.

Section 95 of the CJA requires the Secretary of State to publish information to help courts to perform 'their duty to avoid discriminating any persons on the ground of race or sex or any other ground'. Whether or not the advocate chooses to gently remind the court of this 'duty' is a question of whether or not the issue of race or gender may be made relevant to the circumstances of the offence.

Much should be made of the previous good character of the accused; this applies to both the client and his witnesses. The consequences for the accused's dependents of his imprisonment is also of some relevance. There is little strength in an argument for a return to the family if the wife and children are beaten by the accused. For the same reason the presence and support of the accused's family is helpful. Concentrate on the circumstances of the offence and persuade the court of the accused's remorse, good intentions and willingness to co-operate if, for example, a community sentence is imposed. Since the commonest disposal is a fine it is worth taking instructions on the amount (including possible compensation) which the accused could afford each week. It is also important to understand the method of calculating the new 'unit fines' (Wassik & Taylor (1992) especially para 3.2).On content, see also para 8.8 above, 'lessons from research'.

8.12   Style

8.12.1 Balanced argument

Avoid resting everything on one argument but try to avoid being seen to throw everything in; 'the same old litany of excuses' is not persuasive. Do not adopt automatically any recommendations which appear in reports before the court; be realistic. It may be that the probation officer is inexperienced and is over-optimistic in suggesting probation for the particular offence. Note carefully any questions which the court asks the probation officer; this will often give you an indication of the court's views on sentencing possibilities.

You may lose credibility if you fail to recognise a problem and can independently support an argument for such a result. If you appear frequently in the same court your credibility is a vital asset. It is your professional responsibility to maintain it. You may recognise that the bench would regard a prison sentence as necessary so as to mark the gravity of the offence. Having accepted that premise you can then go on to argue that the sentence should be suspended. Mitigating circumstances can often be woven into a submission based on sentencing guidelines. This will avoid the pitfalls of a presentation which seems all too familiar to the bench.

8.12.2 Attitude

It is obvious that you must appear as if you believe completely in this defendant and in what you say. However, beware conveying the impression that you are 'sympathetic to crime' or a 'defence hack'; avoid slang which suggests a lack of professional detachment from offenders.

8.12.3 Links and phrases

Remember to outline your objective at the start '... Sir, I shall try to persuade the court that a fine would be an appropriate sentence in these circumstances' then move to the circumstances of the offence '... my client accepts that this is a serious offence and sincerely regrets his involvement. However, I think there are several factors which suggest that this is not a case at the higher end of the scale ...'. Then mention any good points in mitigation '... Sir, you will have noted that not only did my client plead guilty but he assisted the police in the recovery of the goods ...'. Conclude by noting your best points and suggesting an appropriate course of action.

8.13   After sentence

It is good practice to explain to your client the implications of the sentence. This may require some anticipation and research on your part. Note that, as from 1st October 1992 the Criminal Justice Act (1991) Part II introduces a new scheme for release from prison on licence. Archbold summarises the period which the offender may expect to serve in prison (see Archbold (1993)). The client may also need some explanation of the practical consequences of the sentence, for example, where to pay the fine, what will happen if it is not paid or if there is a breach of a conditional discharge.

Practice Exercise: Planning a plea in mitigation

Prepare a plea in mitigation based on the following documents. You may find it useful to present the plea, using a colleague as 'judge' and others to observe and offer constructive criticism of your performance.

Y= year : m= month

Assume that the offence was committed in (month 0)

Background

Lorna Bee pleaded guilty in (month 2) at Anytown Magistrates court to a charge of theft from 'Mothers' Ware and Baby Care', a self-service store in the Anytown Shopping Centre. She was observed by an assistant hiding items of children's clothing under a large overcoat. The overcoat was placed over her arm and she carried a plastic bag under the coat. She was stopped just outside the store by the assistant and was found to have an adult's patterned skirt, and two pairs of children's dungarees (age 4-5). The total value of these items was £98 and there were no other items in the bag. The bag itself was from another store in the Shopping Centre. She refused to return to the store and a fracas developed during which she struck the assistant across the face. A security guard from the shopping centre arrived and Lorna was escorted to the manager's office while the police were called.

ANYTOWN POLICE

Convictions recorded against.............   C.R.O. No.....................

Charged in name of........*Lorna Bee*........

Date	Court	Offences	Sentence	Date of release
Y-4	Anytown	Theft	Fined £50 Probation	
Y-2	Anytown	Possession cannabis	Probation	

Pre-sentence Report

to the

Anytown Magistrate's Court

Name: Lorna Bee   Age........*22*..........

Address........................   DoB..*1. 8. 1970*.....

Present Offence(s)   (i) Theft

                                    (ii) Assault

1   Lorna Bee is known to me having previously been on probation for 6 months in connection with a conviction for theft in Y-4 and for 1 year following a conviction for possession of cannabis in Y-2.

2   She is currently living in a flat on the Anytown Estate. The accommodation comprises a sitting room, kitchen and bathroom. Ms Bee sleeps on a convertible bed in the sitting room.

3   Both Ms Bee's parents are dead, her mother dying when she was a child and her father dying 5 years ago. She has a

married sister Gwen who is 4 years older than her and who lives in Nothertown, a fifteen minute bus ride from Ms Bee's flat. Ms Bee is close to her sister who virtually cared for the family after their mother died. Ms Bee had a regular boyfriend whom she stopped seeing in (M-3). In (M-1) she discovered that she was pregnant by this man but she has not told him and has no desire to re-establish the relationship.

4   Ms Bee left school at the age of 16 having gained 4 CSE passes, one at grade 1. She is currently employed as a counter assistant in the delicatessen of 'Grocery Superstore' in the Anytown Shopping Centre. Only part-time work is currently available to her there and she works three mornings a week. Her net pay is £60 per week. She had hoped to obtain full-time employment and has been promised this by the store manager when the next vacancy arises. Her rent, inclusive of services, is currently £25 per week. Her first conviction was for theft from her employer. She is a bright woman who has recently enrolled at Anytown Further Education College to study Law and Sociology 'A' Levels part-time. She is hoping to go onto higher education in due course.

5   This is Ms Bee's third offence. She has previously responded well while on probation. She tells me that she had no intention of taking anything from 'Motherware and Babycare'. She had finished her morning shift and was merely wandering around the shopping centre 'in a kind of daze' before going back to her flat. She says that she has been concerned about how she would provide for her child and was feeling anxious and disorientated that morning. She does not deny that she placed items in her bag or that she intended to avoid paying for these. She was still feeling in a trance-like state when the shop assistant grabbed her arm. She admits that she is impulsive and reacted badly to what she regarded as the unpleasant manner of the shop assistant who was calling her names and pulling her back towards the shop. She deeply regrets her actions. She is anxious and concerned about her pregnancy,

about how she will provide for herself and her baby and how the child's arrival will interfere with her educational plans.

6   A further probation order would provide Ms Bee with the opportunity to closely examine the reasons for the type of impulsive offence within the context of this office's 'Offending Behaviour Group'. A new weekly programme for women starts at the beginning of next month and lasts for a period of six weeks. Individual supervision would subsequently be provided and would provide the support that Ms Bee needs in relation to the birth of her child and encouraging Lorna in continuing her studies.

A suitable community placement would also be available for Ms Bee and after the birth of her child she could be assisted with making suitable childcare arrangements.

1   Present a plea in mitigation based on the brief facts appearing here.

2   Consider what evidence you may wish to call:

    i)   as prosecutor

    ii) as defence advocate

8.14 End of chapter references and additional reading

Archbold M I
(1993)
*Archbold Pleadings, Evidence and
Practice in Criminal Cases*
Ch 5
Sweet and Maxwell

Bartle R P
(1983)
Advocacy in the Magistrates Court
Law Institute Journal Vol 57

Chapman J
(1993)
Interviewing & Counselling
Cavendish Publishing

Emmins
(1992)
Criminal Procedure
Ch 1
Blackstone Press

Fitzmaurice C and
Pease K
(1988)
Psychology of Judicial Sentencing
Manchester University Press

Henham R J
(1990)
*Sentencing Principles and Magistrates'
Sentencing Behaviour*
Gower Publishing Co

Holin C R
(1992)
*Criminal Behaviour: A Psychological
Approach to Explanation and Prevention*
The Falmer Press

Hyam M
(1990)
Advocacy Skills
Ch 4
Blackstone Press

Morton J
(1984)
*Defending: The Lawyer's Practical
Guide*
Ch 8
Derek Beathe Publishing

Napley
(1991)
The Technique of Persuasion
Sweet and Maxwell

Shapland J   *Between Conviction & Sentence: The*
(1981)   *Process of Mitigation*
                           Routledge and Keegan Paul Ltd

Thomas   *The Criminal Justice Act 1991*:
(1992)   *Custodial Sentences*
                           Criminal Law Review

Wassik M and   *Blackstone's Guide to Criminal Justice*
Taylor R D   Ch 1
(1991)   Blackstone Press

CHAPTER

9 Advocacy in Practice 2

Civil proceedings

This Chapter will concentrate on one example of advocacy in civil proceedings; an interlocutory application for judgment in the High Court. This example will be worked through as a simulated application under RSC order 14. All the necessary facts and materials for this exercise are included below.

9.1 Context

An example of a simple interlocutory application is a plaintiff's summons claiming summary judgement on the ground that there is no arguable defence to the claim. Most interlocutory applications are heard by Masters of the High Court or district judges in the County Courts. Like some judges, officials dealing with interlocutory applications can develop fearsome reputations amongst advocates appearing before them. It is sensible to maintain good relations with these officials. It is relatively easy for novices to get off on the wrong foot and for the official's impatience to compound their problems.

In the Queen's Bench Division once actions are assigned to a master, that master will deal with interlocutory applications in that case. Masters cannot grant injunctions and, if an interlocutory injunction is required the application must be to a judge, probably in the judge's chambers. Additionally, there are practice masters on duty to deal with ex parte applications, consent orders and the like.

9.2 Preparing for an interlocutory application

Circumstances will vary between different applications and officials. You may be offered a seat or left standing. Assume you will stand unless invited to sit. Each official may expect the application to proceed in a particular way. Some may ask for affidavits to be read; others may ask to be addressed on particular points. It is important, therefore, to be flexible and adaptable.

Prepare a chronology so that you thoroughly understand the sequence of events and can find relevant details and their place in the story without flicking through bundles of documents. Prepare notes of your main points rather than a speech or series of speeches.

Remember that it is for the party initiating the particular process to 'lead off'. Even where an usher has handed the Master a note of the names of those appearing the opening should effect introductions.

9.3   Simulation exercise

The practical exercise which follows is a simulation of an application for summary judgment in the High Court action. Both solicitors and barristers can attend on such a summons but it is a common advocacy task for solicitors. The exercise will be based on group work. You will need personnel for three roles; the Plaintiff's solicitor, the Defendant's solicitor and the Master.

Each application will take between ten and fifteen minutes to hear. If it appears to the Master that the argument will take longer than this, the summons may be adjourned for a special appointment. The exercise will probably be more successful if there is an opportunity for preliminary discussion of common problems. Depending on the circumstances a group can be divided into three sub-groups, each comprised entirely of people who will play the same role, for example all plaintiff's solicitors. Each group could have approximately 20 minutes for discussion of problems identified in preparation. This is the kind of exercise which can be conducted before a small audience, even if others have to conduct it later; it is beneficial to see how others tackle the same task. Alternatively, assuming at least three groups of three, each participant can adopt another role after each application ie so that Plaintiff's solicitor becomes the Master and so on. In this way each participant will play all three roles.

Having assigned the roles each participant should have an opportunity to prepare. Before the simulation 'the advocates' should conduct the following preparation:

1   Draft an outline of the facts in simple narrative form.

2   Research and relate the law to the issues.

3   Deduce the client's goals by reference to the orders which a Master can make in these circumstances.

4   Identify the best and worst outcomes from your client's point of view and the costs implications of particular orders.

5   Identify the arguments which you will use and which the other side should use at a hearing of this application.

6   Identify procedural or documentary errors.

The 'Master' should conduct the following preparation:

1   Familiarisation with the purpose and broad structure of O.14.

2   Identification of basic procedural requirements.

3   Identification of possible orders which may be made on an application under O.14. and of the possible orders for costs which may follow from each.

4   Analysis of what each party must establish in order to obtain/ resist judgment.

The papers which would normally accompany such an application would be the summons (this would indicate the purpose of the application and the place and time when it will be heard), the writ and acknowledgement of service, an affidavit sworn by the plaintiff in support of the application and usually, an affidavit by the defendant in reply. These affidavits may have exhibits attached to them. Only those documents which are essential to the exercise are included here. You should assume that the plaintiff's affidavit in support of the application is in the standard form and claims that the money is still due and owing, and that the defendant notified an intention to defend the proceedings in his Acknowledgement of Service of the writ.

With this kind of exercise it is difficult to provide confidential instructions for each advocate. You will have to infer these from the circumstances. You should, therefore, be prepared to make appropriate concessions according to your own judgment.

Obviously much will depend on your preparation. One thing which you should prepare to deal with is the costs arising from the hearing of the summons. It is possible that one or other side will be awarded the costs incurred up to the date of the summons or only those costs incurred in connection with the summons. In general, the successful party addresses the court first on the question of costs. Where interlocutory proceedings are inconclusive, costs are usually 'reserved' until a subsequent hearing. The hearing here would be 'costs in cause'.

An application like this draws on the advocate's preparation of the facts, the relevant substantive law and the procedure. It is also an opportunity to practice basic presentation skills. Because the three central characters interact with one other this will test your ability to remain calm, to think of counter-arguments and to pursue your case under pressure. The dates on all papers proceed from day 1 which is the date the defendant placed an order for videos to be supplied by the plaintiff. In reality, of course, the actual date would appear. Please assume that the summons is heard on day 60.

Writ indorsed with
statement of claim

IN THE HIGH COURT   (Year) M. 6735
QUEEN'S BENCH DIVISION

Between

MINIMARK VIDEO SUPPLIES plc   plaintiff

-v-

CHIAN DRASCULA

trading as

CHIANDRAS VIDEO RENTAL   defendant

To the Defendant Chiandras Video Rental of Quaint Alley, Hatfield,
Hertfordshire,

This writ of summons has been issued against you by the above-named
plaintiff in respect of the claim set out on the back.

(Notice as to completion and return of acknowledgement of service).

Issued from the Central Office of the High Court this 49 day of (Year).

Statement of Claim

The plaintiff's claim is for the sum of £25,645.00p being the price of
goods sold and delivered to the Defendant and interest thereon from the
date of delivery pursuant to section 35A of the Supreme Court Act 1981.

Particulars

To goods comprising videos sold and delivered to the defendant (on day
14), full particulars of which have been given to the Defendant by invoice
No 8004.

AND THE PLAINTIFF CLAIMS:

1   £25,645.00p

2   Interest pursuant to the said statute at the rate of 15 percent per
    annum equivalent to the sum of £368.87p for the period from (day 14)
    to issue herein.

3   Interest as above from the date of issue herein at the daily rate of
     £10.54 until judgment or sooner payment.

signed.

If within the time for Acknowledgement of Service the Defendant pays the
amount claimed and £150.25 for costs further proceedings will be stayed.
The money must be paid to the Plaintiff, his solicitor or agent.

This writ was issued by Harmon's, solicitors of 22 Grays Inn Road,
London WC1 on (day 49).

Solicitors for the said Plaintiff whose registered office is 234-244 King's
Cross Road, London NW1.

Defendant's, 1st C. Drascula
Sworn: 50th day Yr 2

IN THE HIGH COURT   (Year) M. 6735
QUEEN'S BENCH DIVISION

Between

MINIMARK VIDEO SUPPLIES plc   plaintiff

-v-

CHIAN DRASCULA

trading as

CHIANDRAS VIDEO RENTAL   defendant

<u>Affidavit of Chian Drascula</u>

Affidavit in reply to

summons under Order 14

I, Chian Drascula, retailer, trading as Chiandras Video Rental of Farm Cottage, near Dearsdan, Hertfordshire, Defendant in this action make oath and say:

1   I have read a copy of the affidavit of Hilary Spondack.

2   For the reasons set out I deny that I am indebted to the plaintiff in the sum of £25,645 claimed in the Statement of Claim or that I was so indebted at the start of this action.

3   I am advised by my solicitor and believe that the statement of claim discloses no reasonable cause of action against me.

4   I am the proprietor of Chiandras Video Rental and Chiandras Videos. Both of these are registered businesses. The former is a video rental shop in Hatfield and the latter is a wholesale business.

5   I did telephone the plaintiff's sales department on the (day 1) and I placed an order for 225 videos, all with different titles.

4   On (day 14) the videos were delivered. My cousin was helping at my warehouse on the Wharton Trading Estate. He took delivery of the videos and signed for them although he did not know that I was expecting to receive them.

5   When he told me the following day what had happened I thought he had made a mistake. It was not until I visited the warehouse 7 days later that I discovered that 2,250 had been delivered. My cousin was unable to find the invoice and so I could not check what had happened immediately. Subsequently I did manage to find it and this is now produced to me marked 'CD1'.

6   On (day 30) I telephoned the plaintiffs' sales department and told them that there had been a delivery error and that they should pick up the videos. I was told that the videos had been delivered and signed for and that, as far as they were concerned, we owed them the money. However, I have never ordered more than 150 videos at one time from the plaintiffs.

7   I immediately wrote to the plaintiffs and a true copy of my letter and of the reply I received is now produced to me marked 'CD 2'.

Sworn by Chian Drascula
on the 50 day of [month]
Year 2 at

Chian Drascula

before

a solicitor/ commissioner for
oaths.

This is the Exhibit marked 'CD 1' referred to in the affidavit of Chian Drascula sworn before me this   day of Year 2.

SALES INVOICE   NO. 8004

CHIANDRAS VIDEO RENTAL

To 450 videos (various titles) as
per your telephone instructions
listed on the accompanying sheets.   £25,645
(inclusive of VAT)

If payment is made within 14 days customers may deduct 10%.

Received in good condition.

R Marted
per C. Videos

This is the Exhibit marked 'CD 2' referred to in the affidavit of Chian Drascula sworn before me this 50 day of Year 2.

Chiandra's Video Rental.

Quaint Alley, Hatfield.

(day 30)

Minimark Video Supplies,
234-244 King's Cross Road,
London NW1.

Dear sirs,

I received an order of videos from you a little while ago. I only just noticed that you have delivered too many videos here and I have to suggest that you should come and take them back. They are all still in v good condition. If you would kindly ring me I will arrange for someone to be at the delivery address to hand them over to you at whatever time is most convenient. I have to say I am sorry that this has happened and hope that we will continue to do business in the future.

Yours sincerely,

C. Drascula.

Minimark Video Retail
234-244 King's Cross Road, London NW1.
(day 32)

Chiandras Video Retail,
Quaint Alley,
Hatfield.   Our ref D/C9276/pd.

Dear sir,

Thank you for your letter dated 23rd (day 30) the content of which is noted. We regret that we must insist on payment within 28 days from delivery as per our standard terms. If you should have any difficulty with this please telephone the writer (quoting the above reference) to discuss the matter further.

Yours sincerely,

P Dickens.
Account Controller

9.4   Evaluating your performance

The following guidance notes are based on the written standards for the Legal Practice Course and include some elaboration of what each may imply in this particular context. One way of evaluating the performance is peer assessment; this can be supported by tutor feedback where available. Probably the most efficient way is for the Master on each occasion to offer constructive criticism of the advocates appearing before him or her during the concluding debrief and feedback stage:

1   'Demonstrate an understanding of the ethics, etiquette and conventions of advocacy'

   •   both advocates address the Master as 'Master'

   •   plaintiff's advocate introduces self and the defendant's advocate and purpose of application. For example:

      'Master, my name is Mr David Wright and I am applying for judgment under Order 14 on behalf of the plaintiff. Ms Amelia Wrong is appearing on behalf of the defendant ...'

   •   plaintiff's advocate hands over writ and plaintiff's affidavit (the summons has already been given to the usher)

   •   plaintiff's advocate inquires whether Master wishes to read papers, have them read, or have main points outlined

   •   plaintiff's advocate introduces plaintiff's case in manner indicated by Master and indicates any errors of substance or form

   •   defendant's advocate responds in like manner (ie by reading Defendant's affidavit or outlining main points)

   •   both advocates respond to any questions by Master

   •   both advocates make a final submission to Master if requested to do so indicating, if necessary, any material matters of fact procedure or law which have not previously been raised

- defence submissions usually follow substantive argument. Plaintiff's advocate makes final submission in response
- master makes an order in relation to substantive issues
- if appropriate both advocates make a submission as to the appropriate order for the costs of the hearing
- master makes an order for the costs of the hearing

2 'Structure and present in simple form the legal framework of the case' and 'structure the submission as a series of propositions based on the evidence'

Each advocate should:

- indicate the legal principle/s which will determine the outcome of the summons
- indicate the material facts
- present the issues for determination in a form which is comprehensible and logical in the context of the particular application

3 'Identify, analyse and assess the specific communication skills and techniques employed by the presenting advocate'

Each advocate should:

- maintain an upright posture unless invited to sit by the Master
- maintain appropriate eye contact with the Master
- indicate the point/s in issue
- speak simply, succinctly and sufficiently to convey their client's case in relation to each point
- recap on points made, questions asked or issues raised as appropriate
- respond cogently to any questions asked by the Master
- be courteous without being ingratiating

- be assertive in conveying the points they wish to make
- resist being badgered into conceding crucial points

See also Chapter 10 at para 10.5 for some further feedback on your conduct of this exercise

9.5   Reading in support of the exercise

Rules of the Supreme Court of Justice (The White Book)

O'Hare and Hill R (1992) - 'Civil Litigation', Longman

CHAPTER

10 Evaluation and Reflection

'*Anybody taught only what to learn has been prepared for the present, which will soon be the past; anybody who has been taught how to learn has also been prepared for the future.*'

Houle (1980)

10.1 Reporting back to your client

When a case has been heard the decision has to be explained to the client. For the solicitor advocate this role is particularly significant. A barrister may be able to explain an adverse decision by witnesses 'not coming up to proof' (not giving their evidence as their proof of evidence suggested they would). A solicitor advocate, on the other hand, may have interviewed the witnesses herself, indeed, she will often have handled the whole case. This underlines the importance of planning and of identifying strengths and weaknesses so that the client knows in advance what the risks are. If the case fails the client should have been warned of the particular risk.

10.2 Continuing to learn from your own experiences

At law school it is relatively easy to obtain constructive criticism of practical performances. The more experienced you become the more difficult it is to obtain good constructive criticism from your peers. If you are to continue to improve at any skill you need critical feedback. Your only resource for self-development may be your own capacity for critical reflection on the things you do. To utilise and develop this resource requires practice, commitment and a very clear idea of both overall objectives and the detailed objective of every piece of advocacy you do. What was my objective in that submission? Did I advance my objective? What was my objective in cross-examining that witness? How did that objective contribute to achieving my overall objective? We all stop improving when we feel smug. Many of us, unless we receive sure indications that our performance is below the mark, may begin to feel smug. How can you avoid this and continue to learn?

10.3   Finding practice exercises

It does not require a lot of careful preparation in order to practise basic advocacy techniques. If you have access to case files of any kind, it is a relatively easy task to take a statement out, assign the role of that individual to one or other of you and conduct an examination-in-chief or cross-examination of that 'witness'. There is a story of a famous American lawyer who conducted cross-examinations of works of art in galleries at weekends, practising organising the sequence and style of questions. In one case his junior counsel had made a poor job of a cross-examination one morning. During the lunch break he had her cross-examine a tree; in the afternoon she was brilliant (she said)!

A lot of ungraded feedback (formative assessment) and repeat performance is necessary before a real improvement in skills is evident. A common problem in skills courses is that tutor feedback is often only given fully and individually at the point of formal assessment (summative assessment). Following assessment there may be few, if any, opportunities to build on the valuable learning experience which summative constructive criticism can provide.

There are many ways of mitigating the problems of limited feedback. The involvement of a tutor is not a necessary precondition of any one of these methods working.

10.3.1 One alone

Speeches and submissions can be usefully practised on your own, preferably in front of a large mirror. This is particularly helpful for getting an impression of body language, especially eye contact. If you can look yourself in the eye for long periods and keep track of your points you will be doing well! Do not be overly concerned about what you see; remember that we are often our own worst critics.

You can also evaluate your own planning by reading case papers and organising issues into suitable sequences. Several exercises are suggested in this book which you might try to work through. Here for example, is a mind map for the issues in the Rouse trial which you should have attempted at the end of Chapter Three.

Mind map of issues in the Rouse trial

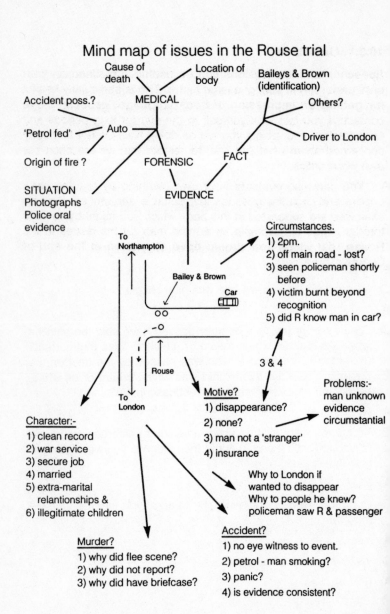

Cause of death

Location of body

Baileys & Brown (identification)

MEDICAL

Accident poss.?

Others?

Auto

'Petrol fed'

Driver to London

Origin of fire ?

FORENSIC

FACT

SITUATION
Photographs
Police oral
evidence

EVIDENCE

To
Northampton

Circumstances.
1) 2pm.
2) off main road - lost?
3) seen policeman shortly
   before
4) victim burnt beyond
   recognition
5) did R know man in car?

Bailey & Brown

Car

To
London

Rouse

3 & 4

Motive?
1) disappearance?
2) none?
3) man not a 'stranger'
4) insurance

Problems:-
man unknown
evidence
circumstantial

Character:-
1) clean record
2) war service
3) secure job
4) married
5) extra-marital
   relantionships &
6) illegitimate children

Why to London if
wanted to disappear
Why to people he knew?
policeman saw R & passenger

Accident?
1) no eye witness to event.
2) petrol - man smoking?
3) panic?
4) is evidence consistent?

Murder?
1) why did flee scene?
2) why did not report?
3) why did have briefcase?

Exercise One

Here is another example for you to think about. In Chapter Four on Planning, there was a section concerned with possible cross-examination strategies in the Peter Hain trial. Here is a small sample of the technique of Lewis Hawser. Hain's counsel started his cross-examination of the first boy as follows:

Q: Are you colour blind?

A: No.

Q: So you know the difference between blue and brown?

A: Yes.

Q: When the events were taking place it was daylight?

A: Yes.

Q: You said the shirt was white with blue checks?

A: Yes.

Q: Others whom the thief actually passed have said the shirt he was wearing was white, cream or off-white. Was that correct? (No answer) If someone who was passed by the thief on the pavement said the thief's shirt was white, cream or off-white, would you agree that was a correct description?

A: No.

Q: When you were sitting outside this court yesterday, you were talking to (boys 2 and 3) about the evidence you were going to give in this case, weren't you?

A: No.

Q: I'll repeat the question, were the three of you together outside this court?

A: Yes.

Q: Were you talking about the case?

A: (Pause) Yes.

Q: Were you talking about when you first joined the chase?

A: Not as far as I remember.

Q: You were, weren't you?

A: I wasn't ... (pause) ... maybe (boy 2 and 3) ...

Q: Were any of you talking about when you first joined the chase?

A: Yes.

Hawser cross-examined the bank teller as follows:

Q: You have just told us very fairly that you must have seen about Peter Hain on television.

A: Yes.

Q: It was clear that you knew Peter Hain had been arrested and charged with this offence?

A: I did, from the radio.

Ask yourself what considerations influence the *future* direction of each of these two cross-examinations and try to outline a plan for each.

10.3.2 One to one

Another important way of continuing to improve performance is to give feedback to each other - one as advocate and the other as witness, judge or Master depending on the nature of the task. The non-advocate can give structured feedback to the advocate according to predetermined criteria. A slight variation on this theme is one to one plus observer/s. This is particularly useful before a formal assessment where you have access to the grading criteria. It also enables you to highlight any problems with criteria which can be explored with tutors before the assessment takes place.

10.3.3 Goldfish bowl

This method of soliciting feedback requires one or two people to conduct an exercise in front of the rest of a group; the performers are in the 'goldfish bowl', the rest outside.

There are potential difficulties with this method. However, it is particularly useful where the group know each other well and have demonstrated an ability to deliver constructive criticism. Usually it is only the most confident and prepared people who are willing to do it; sometimes (but not always) they need the practice the least. The rest are conscious of their own shortcomings and feel unable to comment, particularly adversely. As a demonstration it has value but if the criticism is not skilfully delivered the volunteers may become discouraged.

10.3.4 Group work

This is a variation of the goldfish bowl. For this everyone, except possibly the tutor, gets in the goldfish bowl. It might be used as follows:

Select a performance, cross-examination, for example, and select one student as the witness. Everyone else plays either an examining-in-chief or a cross-examining advocate. Both groups of advocates get into a huddle and decide on an examination and cross-examination strategy. The witness meanwhile prepares for her role, thinking about how she will answer particular questions and thinking about inconsequential background detail for her character (someone good at 'imaging' is ideal for this).

Examination-in-chief is conducted first and then cross-examination. Each advocate conducts the examination of the witness taking up from the place where the last advocate finished. Each advocate finishes at a pre-arranged signal from the tutor. Each advocate is stuck with the mistakes of those who went before. The tutor may decide the cross-examination is such a shambles that you need to start again. In this case you can analyse the errors and discuss strategy changes. As the exercise proceeds, you may want to add an opposing advocate to object and a judge to rule. One advantage of this method is that it involves everyone in planning and delivery. Although involving so many players does not imitate cross-examination in real life, the process is fun and places all participants on an equal footing. This maximises opportunities for learning from one another.

10.3.5 Observation

Another suggestion for improving your own performance is to watch an advocate, either in court or on video, and to analyse her performance. Make notes of major strengths and weaknesses, or concentrate on one aspect of the performance and analyse it carefully.

10.4   Giving and receiving criticism

In my experience as a teacher students give excellent feedback on the content of legal argument but startlingly basic feedback on the skills of presenting that argument. The comment, 'That was very good' is not much use to anybody.

Constructive criticism should analyse the elements of performance one by one according to whatever criteria are appropriate or available. If none are available, it can be a very useful exercise to devise criteria for assessment for yourself. The process of group discussion often exposes different perceptions, helps to isolate those elements of performance which are crucial and encourages people to discuss knowledge or experience which would otherwise remain personal.

Some of us are defensive about taking criticism, particularly when we think it is unfair. Worse, some of us think that our peers have nothing to teach us, particularly if we think they are less able than we are. It is a mistake to hold these attitudes generally and particularly so in relation to advocacy. Anybody, even those unschooled in the law, can tell us if they followed our argument, whether we were fluent, whether we were persuasive. Significantly, only a non-lawyer can give us honest feedback as a juror.

10.4.1 Receiving constructive criticism

If you are on the receiving end of feedback, try to remember the following points:

- use positive body language; for example an open stance (arms unfolded)

- acknowledge fair criticism; remember it is another's perception of you and that you cannot fully appreciate how you are perceived. Ask for clarification and elaboration, for example 'You said that my delivery was too slow; did you feel that was the case all the way through?' or 'What did you think the effect of the slow delivery was in this exercise?'

- do not argue with the person giving feedback; wait until they have finished before deciding whether to respond

- if nothing positive is offered, ask what you did well, ask for comparison with previous performances

- recap on the feedback in full

- thank the person for their feedback; indicate which comments are not accepted and why

- ask for advice on how to improve

10.4.2 Giving constructive criticism

Giving constructive criticism is a highly skilled task. Bear the following points in mind:

- focus on what was observable; do not offer opinions about underlying attitudes or feelings or things which cannot be changed, for example 'You don't seem like a very confident person and you therefore don't come across very well' is poor feedback. The focus of the feedback should be to explain exactly how she did 'not come across' very well'. Was it her voice, words, movement, delivery, or was her style inappropriate for the particular task?

- identify and acknowledge those elements of the performance which were competent or better than competent; give examples of behaviour which were successful

- be honest in offering criticism

- do not be patronising or flippant

10.5   In conclusion: evaluating the Chiandras simulation exercise

In conducting any particular exercise, the issues you raise will be very important. You may be feeling very confident until the other advocate or the Master raises a point you have not noticed. If you cannot respond your level of performance may decline rapidly.

Let us look at the application for summary judgment exercise in Chapter Nine. The following are points you should have considered in the course of your preparation:

- the invoice is signed on behalf of Chiandras Videos, not Chiandras Video Rentals

- the writ includes a claim for interest on VAT

- the defendant admits ordering 225 videos; can judgement be entered for part of the claim?

- there is no time specified for payment (a standard form affidavit in support of the application would merely say that the sum was due and owing). In those circumstances, when would the purchaser become liable to payment?

- there are three possible orders; unconditional leave to defend; conditional leave (say, on payment into court of the sum in issue); or judgment in full

- the order as to costs will depend on the order made on the summons; if the action is continuing the costs of the application may be reserved until the full hearing. Otherwise costs are usually awarded to the 'successful' party.

Analyse the reasons for the decision:

- did you focus on the strengths of your case?
- what was the main reason why the case failed?
- did you correctly identify this aspect of the case as a weakness?
- how did you attempt to mitigate this weakness?
- with the benefit of hindsight, what else should you have done?
- how, if at all, did the other side capitalise on this weakness?
- had you anticipated their argument and their approach?
- what responses did you make to their arguments?
- what indications did you receive that your arguments were heard and understood?
- was the outcome justified given the evidence and arguments presented and the applicable law?
- what can you learn from this encounter? What would you change if you could do it all again?

Finally analyse your own presentation skills:

- was your language assertive?
- did you work from notes?
- were you sincere, coherent, logical?
- were your materials well organised?
- did you cope with interference of the pace and continuity of your delivery?
- did you maintain eye contact?

10.6 End of chapter references and additional reading

Guirdham M and
Tyler K
(1992)

Enterprise Skills for Students
Chs 1,3,9
Butterworth Heinemann

Houle C O
(1980)

*Continuing Learning in the
Professions*
Jossey-Bass

Schein E H
(1971)

*Professional Education: Some New
Directions*
McGraw Hill